101 Ways to Make Poems Sell

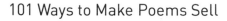

CHRIS HAMILTON-EMERY was born in Manchester ... 1963 and studied painting and printmaking in Manchester and Leeds. In the early 1990s he worked as Design Manager of the British Council and sat on the Council of the Chartered Society of Designers. He joined Cambridge University Press in 1994 and became Press Production Director, leaving to join Salt Publishing full-time in 2002, where he is now Publishing Director. He also works as a publishing consultant with a wide range of clients including Blackwell Publishing, Cavendish Publishing and Polity Press, as well as a number of small literary presses. He was elected to the Board of the Independent Publishers Guild in 2006.

Writing as Chris Emery, his poetry has appeared in numerous journals including *The Age*, *Jacket*, *Magma*, *Poetry London*, *Poetry Review*, *Poetry Wales*, *PN Review*, *Quid* and *The Rialto*. He was anthologised in *New Writing 8* (Vintage, 1999). A first full-length collection, *Dr. Mephisto*, was published by Arc in 2002. A new collection of poetry, *Radio Nostalgia*, is available from Arc. He lives in Great Wilbraham with his wife, three children and various other animals.

WITHDRAWN

1 4 MAY 2023

York St John University

3 8025 00608804 4

Writing as Chris Emery

Poetry
   The Cutting Room (Barque Press, 2000)
   Dr. Mephisto (Arc Publications, 2002)
   Radio Nostalgia (Arc Publications, 2006)

101 Ways to Make Poems Sell

The Salt Guide to Getting and Staying Published

Chris Hamilton-Emery

YORK ST. JOHN
LIBRARY & INFORMATION
SERVICES

SALT

CAMBRIDGE

PUBLISHED BY SALT PUBLISHING
PO Box 937, Great Wilbraham PDO, Cambridge CB1 5JX United Kingdom

All rights reserved

© Chris Hamilton-Emery, 2006

The right of Chris Hamilton-Emery to be identified as the
author of this work has been asserted by him in accordance
with Section 77 of the Copyright, Designs and Patents Act 1988.

This book is in copyright. Subject to statutory exception
and to provisions of relevant collective licensing agreements,
no reproduction of any part may take place without the written
permission of Salt Publishing.

First published 2006

Printed and bound in the United Kingdom by Lightning Source

Typeset in Swift 11 / 16

This book is sold subject to the conditions that it shall not,
by way of trade or otherwise, be lent, re-sold, hired out,
or otherwise circulated without the publisher's prior consent
in any form of binding or cover other than that in which
it is published and without a similar condition including this
condition being imposed on the subsequent purchaser.

ISBN-13 978 1 84471 116 1 paperback
ISBN-10 1 84471 116 1 paperback

SP

1 3 5 7 9 8 6 4 2

For the neophytes,
the grand viziers
and the barbarians
at the gate.

Contents

Acknowledgements

There's no way this book could have been written without the huge input of so many people over so many years, from poets, workshop managers, reviewers, journalists, literary editors, publishers, designers, typesetters, printers—well, the list goes on and on. I've worked with hundreds of authors from around the world, and each of them has taught me what matters about literature. The people I've learned from most are my customers, they've taught me what they want and they've taught me how to sell it to them. Hopefully, I'll continue to do that.

I'd like to thank my wife, Jen, for living with me while I wrote this book, and for trying to juggle Salt, the children, pregnancy and our livelihood. I'd like to express gratitude to Michael Holdsworth at Cambridge University Press, from whom I learnt a great deal about the operations of a publishing business. I'd like to thank my co-directors at Salt, Linda Bennett and John Skelton, for their support and insights. I'm grateful to the Arts Council of England for a grant to develop the marketing campaign for this book.

Finally, I'd like to thank you, the reader, for spending your hard-earned cash on me, and I hope you find this book a welcome addition to the shelves, but one that has its spine broken and Post-it notes hanging from the pencilled margins. This book should be put to use and made to work.

Preface

Poetry is a multi-million dollar, international business, though you could be forgiven for thinking that it was the poor relation of the book trade—the country cousin, buck-toothed and socially inadequate—perhaps a little smelly and stained. Of course, it's true to say that poetry accounts for a very small percentage of the total book buying sales, but it's still a big business. Despite this, many booksellers and literature readers will glaze over and look a little panicked at the mention of the "P" word. One anxiety is about *difficulty*. Poetry is an art form that demands participation and intellectual effort from the reader. Effort is in short demand in an age of passive consumption. This isn't to say that poetry isn't entertaining (it certainly should be), we've just grown lazy about our intake of high culture. As Stephen Page of Faber and Faber succinctly put it, most publishers have "rushed to the middle". The book trade is intensely conservative and slow-moving. The middle ground, middlebrow hegemony in all genres has, at times, looked like stifling creativity and innovation. Poetry has to compete with this if it is to survive in any meaningful way.

Another anxiety is *ubiquity*. Quite literally, thousands upon thousands of people attempt to write poetry, coming into the art at many levels, but mostly as amateurs enjoying the problems and rewards of wrestling with language, capturing emotional extremes and seeking solace and comfort.

Many people will, at a push, admit to *writing* poetry at some point in their lives (usually in their adolescence), but few people would confess to *reading* any in their daily lives, especially the modern stuff. There is nothing fundamentally wrong with this gap, except that so many people want to see their poetry published in a book. This is a great mystery, that thousands of folk believe that their poems *will* be purchased, when so few buy any poetry at all. So, if poetry is a multi-million dollar business, what is selling? Dead poets sell well. Famous poets sell well. The rest is a struggle between tiny quantities and no quantities. Poetry is, it seems, an art aimed at posterity with little contemporary appetite for the new.

Many surveys around the world have shown that trade sales of poetry are in modest decline. There are perennial discussions of poetry's demise, of its retreat into academia, of its neglect of the "general reader". We are offered either resignation or quack remedies. Poetry "cannot be marketed", or alternatively, we are reminded of how the grass roots can really show the best way forward towards a poetry of total inclusion— as if it was all about a form of mass participation in the art. I sincerely doubt that either position is true.

All of this has led to the view that poetry is a "special needs" case, whose only hope of survival is to broaden out, dumb down, and seek patronage and subsidy. Whilst any business needs "seed capital" and investment to build its operations, the poetry business seems to be a permanent charity case—non-profit, beyond the seedy world of commerce and the confections of mass marketing and media giants. Some people will treat it as such. Some will not. Whether you are a publisher or a poet, if you are interested in creating a paying readership for poetry, then this book is for you. This book is about the business side of the poetry scene, about making sales and profits to fund literature in a sustainable way.

I'm not interested in seeing any art form limp along, least of all poetry. If you want poetry to prosper in the twenty-first century, then this book will help you to find a way to make that happen. You could say I am on a mission in these pages, a mission to see the perceptions of poetry realigned, to recognise that a major literary genre can also be a major publishing genre, one equipped with sales to match the aspirations of its practitioners. There's no easy route out of the current predicament. The only way forward is to learn some basic business and marketing skills, and to hustle for all you are worth.

1

Making Poetry Submissions

Before considering making a poetry submission to any publisher, it is important to consider what you want to contribute to a publishing relationship and precisely what you want to achieve within your writing life. This is certainly not a financial contribution, we're not talking about vanity presses in these notes, it is a far more important contribution than just money. Understanding your intentions and efforts as a writer will, to a large extent, determine what choices are to be made and provide you with a few opportunities and very many challenges. It might surprise you to discover that being published may not be the best choice for you and your work.

Why Do I Write?

There are, of course, as many reasons for writing as there are people on the planet, but understanding your desires (or compulsions) as a writer will help you to think through whether you really want to be published and whether you are prepared to work (often exhaustively) to develop a readership for your writing within a commercial context.

Very many people begin to write poetry in their adolescence and many write from experience of trauma, personal loss or as a form of spiritual or emotional growth. Some write from their first experiences of ethical and political conviction. Some from their first reading of a major poet at school; many learn through emulation. All of these are perfectly valid and rewarding pastimes without any form of publication. You may have had a substantial writing life producing poems as an extension of your emotional experience. However, this is not a test for the financial viability of your poems in a published work.

The authenticity of your feelings, their depth, novelty and sincerity, are not markers for commercial success. Many publishers will recognise the characteristics of such poetry and flinch from the memory of heart-felt writing, from young and old alike, which fails to stimulate the reader beyond calls for sympathy. Alas, sympathy does not sell books; it sells greeting cards.

Emotional excess and the unburdening of strong personal feelings can be a major impetus to writing, but this is rarely the sole basis of a successful poem. Some poets do this well, but the measure of their success lies not in the expression of their personal feelings (or their excess), but in how they have engaged the reader and transcended such conditions with new language. In this way, the commercial publication of poetry demands reciprocity and interaction with a readership.

Frequently the reader is a participant in the very process of the poem, active rather than passive. You may be the best reader of your own work, but without someone else, the poem is incomplete, and without a buyer it cannot be published.

Many poets and commentators will correctly state that the writer works first for themselves; there is no doubt that this is true. But as soon as you seek to develop a readership beyond your family, friends and colleagues, you will establish for yourself a set of ambiguous responsibilities. Clarifying and articulating these responsibilities will define your writing. If you want people to pay for your poems, to give up their time and effort in order to engage with your work, then one responsibility is commercial. Why should anyone pay money to read you? More importantly, why do you think that they will? It isn't the publisher's job to answer such questions, it's their job to ask them.

What does Publication Mean for My Writing?

Being published means entering into a partnership with a publisher and commits you to the serious application of your time and talent to finding readers and marketing your work. If you are not primarily interested in helping to sell books, you do not need to approach a publisher, as they almost certainly won't succeed in making sales on your behalf without your active participation. Of course, there are many ways to find readers, and selling books is just one of them. But for publishers who depend on books sales to fund their businesses and develop their relationships with their customers, it is of major significance. Not every book has to be a bestseller; few, if any, will be, but every book, it is hoped, will make a positive contribution to the publisher's financial performance or the cohesion and identity of their list.

This is the commercial publisher's risk: that their often considerable investment in money and human resources will pay dividends in profitable book sales. Where poetry is concerned, those rewards may be very meagre indeed. Most volumes of poetry sell under a thousand copies, many sell less than 300, and some do not sell at all, despite the massive efforts of all concerned.

You may infer from this that commercial publication bears no real relation to the intrinsic value of your writing. It would be folly to merely seek some form of validation through a publishing relationship. Your work may be highly-prized by the publisher as an asset, but it would be wrong to think of the publisher's role as primarily one of defining some true value (though they may try very hard to do so for the sake of their profits). The publisher's primary role is to market and sell books, and to use whatever means are put at their disposal to do so. Good or even great poetry which doesn't sell will not be of much use to the publisher.

At the end of the day, true value is bestowed by a living readership, and publishers need paying customers, here and now, in order to finance their operations. On the other hand, a poet can write rewarding and committed poetry without ever being published in this way, and can, should they wish, self-publish, or indeed find their writing life fulfilled through giving readings and performances in a range of venues and cultural forums. There are many ways to practise poetry, only one of them requires a commercial publisher and that depends on your wish to develop an impersonal readership willing to pay.

What are the Social Conditions of the Poet?

Poetry is a broad church, and more people write it than read it. Even more people read it than buy it. The market for selling poetry is, in relation to the total book trade, an extremely small one, and it is complex, fragmented, well-managed and highly competitive. Because of this, it is notoriously difficult to coordinate a sustainable economic model for contemporary writing. You will be extremely unlikely to earn a living from selling your poetry. However, you may earn money from a range of cultural projects related to "acting" as a poet, and some writers seek to earn their incomes from running workshops or courses, teaching English or Creative Writing, making festival appearances, giving paid readings, taking on residencies, and becoming cultural commentators and critics. Others may seek grants and bursaries or roles within the media.

The range of possible jobs which relate to poetry has in fact become highly professionalised, whilst the task of selling poetry has become more demanding, expensive and sophisticated. Some would say decadent and corrupted. Often the two go hand in hand; selling poetry books depends increasingly on how well the writer is known within a range of often distinct literary communities, some of which may be supported by the public sector and administered by civil servants.

Despite the rapid growth of public sector support within the culture industry, the market for poetry has been in decline. Some consider this to be a feature of the current management, some of its critical reception, others consider this as the negative impact of academic study. Given the huge growth in undergraduate numbers since 1990, it would be inaccurate to state that those of us studying literature are not valid as a readership. Many will go on to a lifelong engagement with, and commitment to, literature.

In the main, this is not a failure of any single party, it is symptomatic of changes in the commercial structure of bookselling in general, and the increasing need for booksellers to generate profits. Poetry is not a mass-market product, even if at times it crosses over into the world of bestsellers. It sells in modest numbers to a highly-informed and often specialised readership. This readership can be extended, and doing so is the problem of poets as much as it is of publishers.

Building a reputation as a poet is a vital feature of having any form of commercial life as a writer. Some may baulk at the notion of working in this way on an art form which is traditionally perceived to operate at a high level, dealing with spiritual, social and political realities. However, this is not the case where publishing is concerned. Anything you do as a poet to manage and extend your status as a writer will be of considerable use to the publisher. Indeed, some publishers will invest a great deal of effort in support of managing and publicising your writing persona, in order to achieve more sales and realise their investment in your writing. Constructing perceptions of the writer and, indeed, their celebrity, can be a full-time occupation for some people within a publishing business. Writers are expected to support this process.

For very many poets, the navigation of literature officers, workshop managers, festival and venue directors, university lecturers, broadsheet literature editors, critics of all shapes and sizes, small magazine editors, listservs, Web masters, librarians and perhaps most troublingly, other poets, can be a demanding daily task. Some poets excel at building such networks of relationships (and their dependencies), others find this repellent and inauthentic behaviour. However, the more experience the poet has of knowing who's who, and who to call upon to further their career as a writer, the more chance they have of commercial success. Some are combative in their pursuit of this, some are jealous of others' share of the limelight, whilst others will deconstruct the field and recognise the signs (I almost wrote sins) of patronage and power. Still, no one has ever been plucked from obscurity by a publisher, inexperienced and ignorant of the poetry scene, its operations, its bias, indeed its enmities, hostilities and prize-fixing glamour, and succeeded to achieve marvellous book sales. Knowing the scene (and being known by it) and establishing your relationship to it are as important as scribbling *vers libre* in the attic, or workshopping quatrains at the weekend writing school.

There can be little doubt that success as a poet involves working within such communities; inside them you will achieve one tier of sales (almost "business to business" in nature), and through them you may reach a wider, more general and anonymous readership. If you know nothing of these communities, a publisher may still be interested in you, but if you understand these communities well and have gained some expertise in working with them, a publisher will see their risk reduced and the possibility of sales increased. As a commodity, you are suddenly more attractive.

Who Buys Poetry?

So far, we've made some observations about the circumstances surrounding the business of poetry. We've eschewed discussions of poetic value, of how good your writing actually is, to consider whether it will in fact sell and what you will do to help drive those sales. We've side-stepped the issue of seeing your work in print—if this was your sole desire, it would be better to spare the publisher's cash and the efforts of their staff, and print the book yourself.

Before you can write you need to read, and before you can read you need to buy (remember that the public lending right doesn't feed the publisher's staff). At this point, let's consider who actually buys poetry.

There are many thousands of poetry publications produced every year around the world (yes, thousands), ranging from the strictly amateur to the corporate window-dressing of publishing conglomerates. Some are given away, some stored under the bed or in the garage, a small percentage are sold direct or even through bookstores.

Take a pencil and some paper and write down everyone you know who buys poetry and ask yourself these ten questions:

1 How do they hear about the books?
2 Which places do they buy them from?
3 Do they buy anthologies or single author volumes?
4 Do they buy works from a particular publisher, or from a range of publishers?
5 Do they buy the works of particular authors, or try unfamiliar names?
6 Do they buy contemporary poetry, or the works of historical authors?
7 Do they shop for poetry regularly?
8 How much do you think they spend on poetry each year?
9 How many poetry titles do you think they buy each year?
10 Why do you think that they buy it?

Now you have your list, ask yourself the same questions.

What can you deduce from this kind of survey? Well, one thing to be aware of, if you believe you are au fait with contemporary poetry, less than 20% of new titles are actually sold in bookshops. Far more titles are sold direct. If this doesn't match your experience, you've missed out on an awful lot of new poetry.

Statistically, most poetry sold in bookstores is sold to women, most of that is sold to people over 50 years of age, and most of that sold has been written by dead authors. But there is little research as to where the other 80% of titles is actually being sold.

Unless you, and the people you know, are buying poetry, there will be no market for selling books. An important lesson to learn in considering making a submission is how committed you are to helping others buy books: furnishing them with your enthusiasm for the art, and convincing them that spending their money on poetry will add value to their lives. Make it your business to increase the size of the market. Without readers, there is no future for publishers, and no room at the inn for you. The more people you encourage to buy poetry, the bigger the potential market for you.

Reading all the Books you have Bought

So you have acquired a few thousand new poetry books for your personal library (just kidding), and are wincing at all the money you have had to earn and spend on this stuff, now let's consider reading it all.

Publishers come in all shapes and sizes; some, but not all, are interested in publishing work which significantly extends poetry. Opinion will be hotly divided on exactly how poetry is to be extended. However, most publishers will agree that new poetry should endeavour to be precisely that: new. It is often astonishing how poorly read aspiring poets are, and how many have failed the first hurdle to rise above their idols and pass beyond emulation into the realms of real writing—writing which has its context in the present, here in this very moment, addressing the current state of poetry and its practice and reception in the broad community of the living art. There ought to be a law about this:

> "Poets are not allowed to submit a new manuscript until they have read two hundred single-author volumes of poetry, published since 1980."

In fact, there ought to be several laws about it:

> "Poets writing in the manner of the nineteenth-century Romantics are advised to seek publishers from the same era."

So many submissions are too derivative to be worth publishing. We've read the originals and don't need a karaoke version of Heaney, Plath or Larkin. Where poetry is concerned, regurgitation never aids digestion.

Perhaps the most frustrating thing for publishers is receiving manuscripts which clearly don't fit their lists, addressed "To whom it may concern" or "Dear Editor". Sending the wrong material to someone you cannot be bothered to discover the name of and expecting some response other than the bin would be testing providence in the best of circumstances. Find out about the publishers you are wishing to submit to, learn about their editors, buy their books, read their poets, and discover for yourself whether your writing might be of interest to them.

Never let your abstract desire to be published rush ahead of the desire to consume other people's poetry. Being a reader is, in fact, far more important than being a writer. Remember to read beyond your own prejudices; the aspiring poet should read everything. Okay, not everything, just everything I publish.

Becoming a Player

The world of poetry is not a world of isolated individual practitioners. Hermits in their caves. If you currently find yourself in this position, you should try to get out more. The world of poetry is a very busy place, filled with a wide range of professionals, most of whom are eager to tell you about their talents.

The world of poetry is not filled with gentle suffering creatures (to call upon Eliot). It is not fair, just, or particularly caring. It can be supportive, but it is not a self-help group. It is not a world based upon power sharing. In fact, the world of poetry can be a bear pit and, like any industry, it is competitive and has moments of confrontation and even dirty tricks. Be prepared to take some knocks along the way.

The most frequent knocks will be rejection. Many poets could paper a bedroom with their rejection slips. You'll receive your fair share of these, too. The source of these will be the magazines you are going to successfully submit to before sending a collection to a publisher.

Spend time getting your poems printed in magazines large and small. Focus on magazines (print and Web) which really matter. Spend a lot of time working out which ones are the best. You'll know that from the contents as much as by the list of poets printed in the contributor notes. Building a pedigree as a writer is vitally important, and it will help a publisher to contextualise your work, and even to discover it. Search out magazines, subscribe to them and support them—they are the scouts and trackers of the poetry world, discovering and often nurturing new talent.

Another important feature of succeeding as a poet is to write reviews. Engaging with other work and actively reviewing it is a great way to build your own experience of poetry, its cause and effect, and you won't want to waste your time reviewing material you don't engage with—even if that engagement is intense dislike. Set your sights high. Aim to be a feature writer for *The Guardian, The Boston Review,* or *The Age.* No point spending your expensive time writing reviews for venues with no readership. You may not be successful in placing reviews and finding a sympathetic literary editor, but there's no harm in testing your mettle in the best forums. Above all, ensure your work and where it appears builds your credibility as an expert. Glorious amateurs aren't required.

A side-effect of such endeavours is that the poetry you believe matters will eventually be given air space. Many poets continue to write reviews and serious criticism for precisely this reason; maintaining their position as experts and defending the poetry they want to succeed. They are building ramparts around the castle. If you don't like what's on offer, you'll need some siege equipment and a tactical plan of action.

50 Dos and Don'ts

That's enough background. Let's take a look at the dos and don'ts of preparing a submission:

1 First off, read submissions guidelines carefully. Many publishers don't currently take submissions and find their poets from out in those literary communities you're going to spend your time discovering and playing a part in.

2 Don't ask for feedback on your poems. It's not the publisher's job to act as your advisor.

3 Don't write to ask for submission guidelines. Check the publishers Web site for details. If you haven't access to the Web, go to an internet café.

4 Do check whether a publisher is currently accepting submissions, Web sites often give detailed information.

5 Make yourself a player. A mover and shaker. If you are out there participating in literature, publishers will notice you.

6 Keep submission letters brief. Editors are ferociously busy people. Spend time planning what message you want to get across, and take time to ensure you've got it down in writing, clearly and concisely.

7 Be completely familiar with the publisher's list. If you haven't bought any of their books, why should they bother to publish you? And don't get caught out pretending.

8 At the same time as planning a submission, prepare a marketing plan for how you will personally promote your book. That's for the publisher when you get accepted.

9 Make sure you include your magazine publishing history, citing where and when your poems have appeared.

10 Find out the name of the person you are submitting to. Find out what they like. Find out where they live. Follow them to work. Alright, just kidding, but find out their name.

11 Don't threaten the editor, or be overly familiar.

12 Don't set deadlines for responses.

13 Avoid the common pitfall of purchasing a book as a form of making a submission. Editors can be bought, but only for six figure sums involving a contract of employment.

14 Avoid portentous, weighty titles: "The Succulent Dark of My Fading Time," "Dread Fires of The Iron Soul," etc., are sure to raise the hackles of every editor.

15 Don't spend time explaining why your work is important.

16 Don't justify your work through a negative reading of contemporary poetry. "All this modern poetry is just rubbish; please find enclosed my 20,000 line *Life of Hephaestus* written in Alexandrines."

17 Do check your spelling. Especially the words you think you know how to spell.

18   Do take care with punctuation, and take special care with apostrophes.

19. Echoing Raymond Carver, "No cheap tricks."

20. Avoid sending poems on the death of your cat, mother or Biology teacher. Or how crap your life is. Or about bee-keeping.

21. Beware of sending poems which contain wild metaphor, clever descriptions of everyday phenomena, and make novel use of dialect and idioms, all ending with a stunning epiphany. It's a tired old template now. Descriptive writing can be very dull.

22   Poems on the wondrous nature of God's creation aren't.

23   Manuscripts containing helpful marginal notes about what you are meaning at this point, or how to typeset the stanza or line are profoundly annoying.

24   Avoid hyperbole, cliché, saturated adjectives, and extended simile. High-powered writing is never weakened by such features. Precision is everything in writing, even being precisely vague.

25   Learn the rules in order to break them.

26   Do break the rules. We are all so bored of the rules, especially the ones taught to you on writing retreats.

27   An aside, if someone talks to you about finding your "voice," they're trying to sell you snake oil.

28   Do not centre on the page everything you write.

29   Do not set the whole manuscript in italics.

30   Do avoid fads, like workshop poems in strict forms— sonnets, villanelles and sestinas can be truly

marvellous, but writing exercises rarely make for saleable goods.

31 Do not put © Copyright Denise Cuthbert 2005 on the bottom of every page. No one, especially the editor of a publishing house, is going to abuse the rights to your poems.

32 Do send an envelope big enough to use to send your manuscript back to you.

33 Do supply full postage or international reply coupons, if accepted by the country you are submitting to.

34 Do not set the manuscript in 18 point bold Helvetica. Choose a font that looks like a book typeface in the appropriate size and weight.

35 So many people write on 8.5 × 11.5 inch or A4 paper that they forget that most trade books are around 5.5 × 8.5 inch or 216 × 140mm in format—be aware of the likely size of the printed page.

36 Don't ask for a receipt for your manuscript.

37 Don't ring up chasing progress the week following your submission. Be patient. Publishers accepting manuscripts may receive several hundred per week. Even working 12 hour days no editor can keep pace with the deluge of submissions.

38 If rejected don't waste time demanding to know why. Dust yourself down and move on.

39 Do mention if you have been recommended by another poet from the list.

40 Don't name drop unless the names explicitly bear upon the nature of the submission.

41   Don't waste time sending expensive bound volumes of
     your work.

42   Do send a sample of six to ten poems.

43   Do send some brief endorsements or review quotes,
     but not those from your mother or English tutor.

44   Don't handwrite your letter to the editor.

45   Don't handwrite the poems.

46   Don't include your photograph—especially the moody
     one with the Fedora.

47   Do spend time researching and planning your
     submission. Choose the best poems to suit the
     publisher's list.

48   Don't let a friend or family member submit on your
     behalf. They're your poems, have the conviction to
     make their case.

49   Do tell the publisher why you think the poems will
     suit their list.

50   Finally, don't give up hope. If you believe in your
     writing, keep on reading and developing your skills.
     Keep on building your profile. Spread your
     enthusiasm.

In this chapter, you've learned about what publishing (as
opposed to literature) is primarily about: selling books and
making profits. You've learned that you are an active participant in that process. You may be a novice right now, but by the
end of this book, you'll be on your way to becoming an expert.
Back in point 6 of my "dos and don'ts," I spoke of preparing a

marketing plan, the 101 items in the rest of this book will help you to prepare it and to carry it out.

2

Building your Profile

You may have spent a great deal of time considering how to get into print, especially if you read the first chapter of this book. You may have spent a small mortgage on attending courses and workshops, even degrees and MFAs, to improve your writing. You may have spent half your life developing your critical thinking—firming up your grasp of post-structuralist theory, the Frankfurt School, or ideas of rhizomes, semiotics, fields, *ostranenie*, simulacra and simulation. On the other hand, you may want to invoke some demons, call upon the Muses, entertain, shock or enlighten; make things real and create some "stays against time" within the chaotic, if shared world, of language. Let's take all this as read.

As a poet, there's little doubt that you will have invested enormous amounts of effort into the consideration of the social, aesthetic, psychological and political context for creating your works, building those systems of constraint from which your authentic art will emerge violently into the world. However, it is extremely unlikely that you will have spent any time whatsoever, not one single day's labour, to write a marketing plan for your poems. Why is this?

Perhaps you imagine that your poetry will find its own way into the hands of eager and devoted readers. Worse still, perhaps you imagine that there is, actually, no one to read your work—which begs the question of why bother seeking publication in the first place? Maybe you think that the job of selling books is someone else's problem, or that it's all a rather tawdry affair? You may even think that poetry cannot be marketed, that it surpasses (or bypasses) any notion of commerce, currency and capitalism—or at the very least, resists it with gritted teeth.

Throughout history, poets have often been at the vanguard of new ideas, of new politics, of new nations—even of the barricades on the night of the revolution. Before we start on our survey of selling poems, let me say that the purity of the art will not be compromised in this book. In fact, this book has nothing to say on the value of poems. There are plenty of great books elsewhere which deal with this. This book is about selling poems. Selling your poems.

No book should be deprived of its readership, the job of this book is to offer you some straightforward and practical help to work with your publisher to drive sales. It will help you to define your responsibilities to your audience, and be a test of your commitment to your own writing. One thing for sure, if you thought that the hard part of being a poet lay in the writing process, think again.

 Building your audience is *your* problem. You'll need to graft to achieve a readership. You'll need to work with both hands (and both lobes of your brain) at the same time. You'll need to be tireless in caring for your readers, working day and night to keep them reading. As Philip Larkin remarked: once in the ring, you need to keep throwing punches. In fact, no day will go by without some action on your part to sell your book.

1. Building your Snail Mail Contacts

Working with and through people is *everything* for the writer. Writers and readers form constellations, and those systems need some rules. If you want people to be interested in your writing, you'd better show some interest in people. Love it or loathe it, building relationships on as wide a basis as possible is an important factor in having a writing life. It goes without saying that the work you put in to finding people should result in a large collection of contacts.

Your personal address book, Filofax, Rolodex, PC contact manager or PDA ought to contain at least 200 people you will want to buy your book. Make every attempt to keep a note of birthdays, anniversaries, and important events in the lives of those you come into contact with.

If you are really savvy, keep a note of when you last contacted someone and make a point of staying in touch at least twice a year. A short note, a postcard or gift will remind you of your circle and remind them of your presence, your commitment and your writing. Your focus must always be outwards, never inwards, always on giving something and never getting something out of your contacts. Taking time to stay in touch will pay huge dividends when the time comes to let people know of your latest book.

2. Building your Email Contacts

Email presents one of the most powerful and cost-effective ways to reach an audience and create some word of mouth. There's no doubt that email has done more to open up poetry communities than any other medium.

Unlike blogs, email is a *conversation*, so expect some feedback and handle it professionally. Email is social and ubiquitous. Thousands of poets stay in touch by using email everyday: launching campaigns, politicking, enlisting support, getting news and views, as well as trying out new writing among their peers. It's an almost essential part of every poet's life, and you should aim to build a list of email contacts and stay in touch with people on a regular basis. Aim to pull together at least two hundred personal email contacts. Be promiscuous, supportive and proactive. Introduce yourself to new writers, friends, critics and allies. Remember that the people who end up in your contacts list or address book shouldn't be considered as your personal marketing list, they are people who are interested in *you*, because you are interested in *them*: their beliefs and their work.

A note of warning here, despite the widespread use of email, everyone hates spam. Spam is email sent *en masse* to people who have not requested it. Some people will make it their personal mission in life to actively prevent spam, reporting anyone who sends them unsolicited email. Be careful whose email address you add to your address book. There's a subtle line to be drawn between harvesting addresses to send unwanted adverts about your latest work, and sharing and participating in a support structure. If in doubt, write to ask a potential recipient if they'd like to receive news about your writing. It's also worth remembering that support is reciprocal. Be prepared to help others market their work, and offer to do so. Avoid sending bulk emails where possible and send individual emails out to your friends.

The most important thing about email is its speed and its potential for the "viral" dissemination of news. Nothing sells books better (or faster) than word of mouth and there's currently nothing faster for promulgating news than a well-aimed email.

Make sure that you categorise your email contacts, not everyone will want to receive information in the same way. Categorising your contacts will allow you to filter information as your prepare to send out news. Take care to prepare emails for different audiences. This brings me to another note of caution. There is no tone in an email. Being funny, ironic, provocative or just playing *Advocatus Diaboli* can end up causing major upset, so be careful about what you say and how you say it. Above all, take time with an email which is intended to offer news of your work. Because email is fast as a medium, most people write it in haste. Where your book is concerned, this is a bad policy. Take time over the wording. Prepare a draft and come back to it a few hours later. Fresh eyes always help to spot the glaring error, or improve the impact of the message.

3. Local Reading Venues

Poetry is an art that operates on a fantastic range of levels. You may at times feel as if you've just accepted the latest offer of a permanent home at the local asylum; you may be a little disturbed to find that many of your colleagues in the world of poetry are, well, a little strange. The kind of folk who might spend the day having a good shout at the ducks in the park, or sorting their collection of clothes hangers. The world of poetry is a world of zealots and acolytes, and occasionally, in the mix, you can find someone who runs a truly marvellous local reading venue. These people are nearly always unpaid, hard-working and devoted to entertaining a well-defined local audience. Most cities support such venues. Find the closest to you and pay it a visit on a regular basis. Become known.

Remember that many people have deep-seated aspirations to write poems, even if they would never dream of seeking to be "a poet". Lots of reading venues try to support "names" with unknown local voices, striking a balance and supporting the development of local writers.

Local events can be the fastest way to forge new relationships and to find like-minded people. A committed reading venue can be an oasis when you're striving to test out a new collection. Your local library will have a list of local reading venues. You can almost certainly find out about them online, too, or from the Poetry Society in the UK and USA, and the Poetry Australia Foundation, as well as many other online directories.

Most local reading venues are run by a few core people. Get involved and offer your support. But most of all turn up to the events on a regular basis and get to know people and the poets.

4. Working with your Local Newspaper

It's worth devoting time to building a relationship with your local newspaper. For example, you might offer to write a column for them on poetry and local events.

You might offer to select a weekly poem for them. You might offer to list gigs and events in the region. You might act as the unpaid journalist covering performances and new publications in your area. You could offer to write an article once a week.

Pop in to see the local journalists and have a chat with them. You may be surprised at the response. Feed them your enthusiasm and give them an offer they can't refuse: free copy on things that matter in the world of "high culture and low life"— or "low culture and high life"—take your pick.

Acting as the local correspondent on poetry and performance will almost certainly place you in the centre of the game. Use that position with great care. This isn't about selling your work, but positioning yourself as the expert. Your expertise is the thing which will open more doors, and before you know it you will be on panels and on-call as the specialist in the field. A good local column can be a great proving ground and lead to a vast range of new opportunities. Get involved.

5. Working with Local Radio

Just as working with your local newspaper can help create a forum for you to extend your work as an expert, local radio can provide the same opportunities, but with one significant advantage: poetry is an oral art form and lends itself to radio more than any other medium. The spoken word is compelling, intimate and totally engaging.

A good performance on radio can be spellbinding. If you can find a way of introducing strong performances on your local radio you will find a winning combination for stimulating sales. Talk to your local station and suggest a regular filler between programmes, or a feature in someone's show, where you can surprise and discover a fresh audience for your writing.

Radio depends on character of voice. Lifeless monotone performances don't work. Nor do shrieks. Well, not most of the time. If you scream down the mike, the sound engineer will saw your ears off. If you are unencumbered by personality, then radio isn't for you. But if you enjoy performing, get on the phone and check out the local stations for interest.

Timing is often critical with local radio and finding the right moment to approach a station is often crucial to getting some air space. There may be a local festival, or a national poetry day. Look for the times when an approach may be most fruitful.

There has been a revolution in local broadcasting, brought about by streaming shows on the internet. Tiny stations suddenly have the opportunity to reach mass audiences. A huge number of underground stations have emerged and are busy developing exciting, diverse and rewarding programmes.

It's worth seeking out these tiny independent and fugitive stations to see if there's anything you can do to support the programming.

6. Awards

In separating out awards from competitions, I'm making a distinction between submitting unpublished poems and submitting published collections. The annual awards given to poetry books are often the by-product of private sector companies, foundations and other institutions interested in tax breaks and the culture industry—often with positive intent. For example, the Forward Prize in the UK is assisted by WPP (one of the world's leading communications services groups), who own the Forward Group. Check out the businesses behind awards.

In many cases, prizes are often used to *position* a writer in a sphere of influence, in a *field* as Bourdieu would have it, managing a set of relationships and indeed, the reception of the art, controlling not only who wins, but the means by which they have won and the views people may have of the value of winning. It's in this context that awards matter. Awards construct a realm of understanding, built upon exclusivity and the reflection or consignment of status and value.

Remember that we're building your "profile"; awards aren't about artistic merit, they're about branded consumption. It's not uncommon to find a cluster of poetry presses surrounding and nurturing particular awards, to raise their credibility from the mass of other examples, and then to work with the funders and sponsors to create a platform for the launch of new talent. Talent they have invested in. For example, the Forward Prize produces an annual anthology published and distributed by Faber and Faber.

The defence of awards can be fierce, given that so much time and effort has been invested in them to raise the value of their brand. If you don't like what's on offer, consider the development of your own awards. That might sound a little ostentatious or just plain daft, but every award started sometime (and some of the best have no cash value to speak of—the value of the prize lies in its perception). Nothing on the scene is a permanent fixture and you shouldn't be scared of developing new structures, finding sponsors, like-minded publishers, developing a separate and competing vision of poetry and defining its celebrants. Awards do have an impact on the general public and their primary value lies in long-term sales development, expressed in terms of the fame of the winners. Winners who disappear tend not to sell. An award is a springboard from which you can reposition yourself as a player; a player with new found status. It's imperative, once you've won, to stay in the public eye for as long as possible.

It won't take you long to research the best awards to submit your book to. Work with your publisher at identifying these, plan which awards to target, and plan the timing of your publication to meet the criteria. It's sometimes prudent to delay your publication to ensure you have a clear chance.

7. Using Listservs

Listservs are virtual communities serving emails to a subscribing membership. Unlike bulletin boards, they work through the shared receipt of email from everyone in the community. Some listservs are monitored, some are not, but all work on the principal that you are signing up to a set of rules and responsibilities to share in debate about a set of well-defined concerns, issues or practices.

Listservs have a lifespan and are organic. Communities come together, engage with each other and sometimes disagree, exploding into new communities. The tendency is for listservs to fragment, or to undergo a form of secession, with groups dividing, sometimes violently, as debate heats up or villains turn up to spoil the fun. Listservs all determine their own culture; some are tolerant, whilst others are militantly defensive of any break in decorum. They are fascinating social microcosms. There is frequently a core membership who may have developed the idea for the list, and there is a list administrator or occasionally a small team of administrators. The style of management varies with each list, but most administrators have a light touch and try to preserve the integrity of the list, keeping people on topic and preventing any abuse.

Once you are on board, you can introduce yourself, ask questions and explore issues you share with the list. You could join as a "lurker", hanging around in the shadows, listening in to the conversations, but given we're trying to sell books here, your plan must be to play a part and find some customers. The best way to do this is to join in the debates and find out about everybody. If people share your concerns and approaches to poetry, then let them know about your work and about your book. However, do your groundwork first. The important thing here is to have an active relationship with the community.

There are many mailing list services on the Web and you can search for lists which might interest you, locate the membership page and join. Be aware that some lists can be very fertile and you may receive hundreds of emails on a wide range of topics or "threads". Most listservs provide a range of commands for interrogating archives, list membership and other features. If you are permitted, always review the membership to see who you are talking to.

The most positive thing about lists is that people are usually more than happy to offer advice and support. You will quickly discover if you have any affinity with a list—and vice versa. There are rarely any constraints to joining a listserv; many allow you to join immediately by submitting your email address to the list host. Some administrators may vet membership and ask a question or two about you, but most offer instant access. Search the archives to get a feel for the list and see what issues have been discussed.

8. Building your own Web site

Building a personal Web site can be free and it is easy to develop skills in writing HTML, which is the code in which Web pages are written. Many sites offer simple HTML editors as part of their services and the cost of a Web presence may simply be a banner advert on your home page. Yahoo! Geocities is a good example: http://geocities.yahoo.com/ and there are many other free Web hosting services, like Tripod on Lycos: http://www.tripod.lycos.com/. If you want to take things further, you can register a domain name and buy hosting services to mount an ad free site which is entirely under your control. More on this down below.

It is almost a requirement these days for poets to have a personal Web site, which may feature news on their titles, updates on current projects, readings, tours, pictures and reviews, as well as biographical information. Setting up a site can be as simple or as complex as you want to make it, but this book places considerable emphasis on using the World Wide Web to build audiences and readerships, so let's dwell on this important item.

What makes a good Web site? You can buy a lot of books to find out about this, and I won't dissuade you from doing so. Here are my personal thoughts. On the Web, presentation is critically important as many people are extremely Web savvy and the tolerance for poorly-designed sites is very, very low. Your site should (of course) look professional, but design should play a key role in the preparation of the site. Design is critical.

Your site should be feature rich. It should contain visual and textual information. It should be coordinated, planned, have clear and understandable structure and, most importantly of all, provide the user with some degree of interaction or provide a vital resource. Considering what services and products you offer is extremely important in determining how the site will be structured and how users will navigate through the pages. Plan your site carefully in advance of building it. Organise the structure of the files into directories as you would your PC or Macintosh. Separate files out into image directories, and directories for the content. Organisation will pay off in maintaining and updating your site.

Why make the site interactive? Because it is this feature that will keep people coming back to your site. It is the interactive nature of the Web that differentiates it from other forms of media. The form of interaction can be extremely diverse, from offering links to allowing reviews to be posted, polls, questionnaires and random features. Users may wish to search the site, make choices about what to view and select items of interest. Some may want to play a part, posting information of their own, entering links, posting news. When planning your site, make a development plan as to where you will take it over the course of a year. Is the site going to be about you and your work, or sell your books, or promote you as a class tutor and visiting lecturer? What are you offering readers?

Here are some features to consider:

1 Information on how and where to order your book(s), with links to online bookstores.
2 A biographical note including photographs of you.
3 An events calendar, giving the dates of your readings and the events you are attending.
4 A news page.
5 A links page (offering link exchanges).
6 Essays and articles.

7   Reviews and endorsements of other poets, as well as their comments on your work.

8   A poetics statement and some links to others.

9   Contact information.

10   Information on your publishers.

11   A daily poem.

12   Variable content (items which change randomly upon each visit).

9. Visiting Hours

Web sites are shy creatures in spite of the technocratic onslaught; they lie in wait like trapdoor spiders. They are reactive in nature. All the loud clothes, bells and whistles and general hoopla doesn't work without an audience, and audiences need to be arranged, cajoled and drawn in to the festivities. In order for your site to work, you must act as a representative and go and drum up some business. Web sites don't advertise in a traditional sense as they cannot enter the customer's perceptual space in the way that other media do.

Include your Web address on *everything* you publish: letterheads, business cards, leaflets, email, curriculum vitae, submission letters, grant applications. Leave flyers with local reading groups, independent bookstores, local libraries, poetry libraries, arts cinemas, galleries—any arts institution, and when giving readings, ensure you tell people about your site and explain what is on offer. Make sure you are clear about what the offer is. It's the offer, its quality and the differentiation from other offers that will keep people coming to read about you and what you have to say.

It's vital in the quest for more sales to increase the number of visitors to your site and the quantity of things they can see when they visit. If you have a crude and simple Web site, with little to do, you are almost certain not to develop repeat visits.

10. <A> Stands for Anchor (Linking on the Web)

Links drive the Web. Exchange links with as many other sites as possible. Spend a few days searching out sites you think are relevant to your writing, especially your latest book, and write to site owners to ask them to take part in a link exchange; few will refuse. Links are the lifeblood of the World Wide Web and the whole revolution is characterised by indexing and cross-reference.

Join Web circles, mutual linking engines which drive surfers randomly from page to page and site to site. Join directories, writers' listings, guides, and look out for portals dealing with poets, like the Electronic Poetry Center at SUNY Buffalo.

Your page ranking in online search engines will be influenced by how many people are linked to your Web page. If you want to push your site up the charts, obtaining links is critical. You could set aside one day a month for link development. Researching places to link to will also provide you with new potential contacts and collaborators.

As the heading for this entry says, <a> stands for *anchor*, the HTML tag which provides a Web link, for example:

<a href="http://www.saltpublishing.com">Here we go, off to the Salt Web site!</a>.

If you have never written a Web page, this linking tool is a cornerstone of cross-referencing. The <a> is also known as an "element" and in our example it has an "attribute", an "href" or hypertext reference. The "href" contains the address of the destination, otherwise known as a URL, Uniform Resource Locator. So, now you know. This isn't a technical book, but if there's one skill which can help you to get more from the medium of the age, learning how to write HTML is it.

11. Readings at Bars, Pubs and Private Venues

The audience for poetry must be built up reader by reader. There are now no public forums dedicated to poetry recitals. Here is a warning from Pliny:

> This year has proved extremely fertile in poetical productions: during the whole month of April, scarce a day has passed wherein we have not been entertained with the recital of some poem. It is a pleasure to me to find, notwithstanding there seems to be so little disposition in the public to attend assemblies of this kind, that literary pursuits still flourish, and men of genius are not discouraged from producing their performances. The greater part of the audience which is collected upon these occasions seat themselves in the antechambers; spend the time of the recitation

in talk and send in every now and then to enquire whether the author is come in, whether he has read the preface, or whether he has almost finished the piece. Not till then, and even then with the utmost deliberation, they just look in, and withdraw again before the end, some by stealth, and others without ceremony.

Letters of the Younger Pliny: Book One: Letter 13: To Sosius Senecio

Each reader is precious and each reader offers a potential referral. Finding new readers can be a full-time occupation, and like cold calling, is not for the faint-hearted. Whatever you do, don't drink. Stay in control of yourself, be pleasant and professional.

It's important to accept paid or unpaid readings at every possible venue to try and develop your audience, but plan ahead and treat the audience in the manner it expects. A great deal of underground poetry happens in pubs, which may have been commandeered for some alternative cultural activity. Check out your local area for clubs, bars, beer kellars and other private venues which host poetry events. Get on the mailing list and stay in touch with the host, go to the events and support the administrators. Offer to help to put on an event, and use that opportunity to build more support for the venue, as well as extending your own reputation as an MC.

You will almost certainly grow out of readings in venues of this kind, and they can be exhausting when run late at night. However, the organisers of these reading venues can be tireless supporters of poetry and its reception. Don't expect to sell books at the event, but do take along some flyers or photo-copies giving order details and where to buy.

If you attend a reading and are receiving a nominal fee from the crowd—passing the hat at the end of the night—offer the reading fee to the MC to finance future readings. Get the email addresses of the hosts and make sure to send a note thanking them for their support. Don't forget to ask for feedback on your performance, and listen to it.

12. Readings at Local Poetry Groups

Almost every town and city has a local poetry group and larger cities may have a host of Poetry Groups, each with a cabal at the centre which make things happen and a small base of supporters who attend, often for many years. Where you can, offer to attend to give a reading. Most will be interested in accepting the offer, and almost everyone will want to know how you got published.

Reading at a poetry group can be . . . unusual. There's bound to be someone there with one ear, a slow eye or an abiding interest in the astonishing breadth of DIY adhesives. Be patient with poetry groups and tolerant of the people, their excesses and eccentricities.

Not all poetry groups can be found on the Web as the culture, by and large, pre-dates the internet, so be careful to look up such groups at your local library.

13. Readings at Open Mic Sessions

Many bookstores, and Borders in particular, run Open Mic sessions for local poets each month. Attend any local Open Mic sessions, give the MC your name and read from your book. Take flyers with you for ordering and at the end of your session, show the book and ask anyone interested to approach you for order details.

Remember that most bookstores now benefit from centralised purchasing for almost all of their stock—there's occasionally some flexibility for local publishing, but not enough to warrant a sales push from you or your publisher. There'll be little chance of getting your book on to the shelves in the stores as a result of any Open Mic session. However, a good reading and some schmoozing *can* lead to orders being taken in the store. Open Mic sessions can also be run at poetry cafés and other venues. Surf the Web for your local venues.

14. Readings at Universities

Literature and Creative Writing continue to be massively popular subjects at university and more and more opportunity is being created for further study. Through increasing the number of student places and the range of courses on offer, universities and colleges have recognised the revenue generating power of such degrees or modules, especially with the extension of Creative Writing departments at undergraduate and postgraduate level. Not long ago such courses were scoffed at, but universities are promoting them in terms of the development of problem-solving and life skills, with a slant to the world of corporate communications. Few would support the view that Creative Writing courses produce an output of new literary stars—this being self-evidently untrue. However, the culture of such courses has created a new tier of teaching opportunities and a vocabulary and professional structure which can appear closed and self-perpetuating. Some would argue that it is self-serving and incestuous.

At one level, our literary readerships are becoming institutionalised as the young increasingly encounter literature within an academic context. Dealing with the relocation of literature within the university system is an important issue. It is both unavoidable and not altogether desirable that so many experiences of literature should be framed from a practitioner perspective. The democratisation of literary participation and consumption presents some interesting challenges for publishers and experienced writers alike. However, writing practice, when combined with advanced reading skills, does provide a welcome theatre for new poetic ideas and new poetic product. Let's face it, art schools have been dealing with this for years.

An entire pedagogy is emerging to support the new courses and writers can earn money by both reading and supporting workshops within universities and colleges. Many writers are persuaded of the stability of campus life and more and more are situated within this framework of institutions, visiting fellowship and writers' networks. The best sources of information on this culture is the Association of Writers and Writing Programs in the USA and the National Association of Writers in

Education in the UK. The AWP and NAWE both allow membership and provide information on a vast range of institutions and those who work in them. Many writers move around the circuit as a result of referrals and friendships struck up at conferences or on panels. For some, this is the way in which they earn their livings. Consider joining a "trade body" and ring your local university to find our more about their programmes and events—who runs them and where they are held.

When giving readings within a university context, every department is different. Some may interpret a reading purely in terms of literary theory, others may concentrate on the psychology of readerships. Prepare in advance and try to talk to students, one to one. Remember that students will soon be converted into the literate general public.

15. Giving Interviews

Interviews hold a fascination for almost everyone, whether it be a vox pop insight to life on the road, or the highs and lows of celebrity marriage; people love reading about the world of others. Voyeuristic, brutally-honest or banal, we don't mind, whether it be ten simple questions, or a ten-thousand word investigation into the importance of fish imagery in your third esoteric collection, we love reading interviews. Still, lightness of touch can mean everything. Some interviews extend into lengthy written exchanges which can become solipsistic and narcissistic, interviewer and interviewee outdoing each other in the smart arse leagues. This is sadly often a symptom of the male poet interview. But we still read on, although with a smile of recognition. The best interviews are those which are unguarded and free from the pressures of brilliance and intelligence. Writers don't have to be the smartest kids on the block.

When forced to conduct a written interview, try to follow the narrative path of natural speech—speak your answers out loud and capture the hesitancy and fluidity of your natural voice.

16. Collaboration

There are two types of collaboration, firstly the collaborative "work", which can cement a friendship, help find new trajectories as a writer and open up your writing practice to new and unexpectedly rich veins beyond the limits of self and life writing. However, when trying to sell collaborative works, your sales team will not be wanting to mine those veins, but slash their own. Literary collaboration rarely, if ever, sells well and often comes to represent a disappointment of ambition.

The second type of collaboration is communal promotion and publicity, working with your colleagues and competitors to reach a wider readership. This might include:

1   Running a shared reading scheme around the country
2   Running multimedia events, with film, music and poetry performance
3   Running small festivals, symposiums and conferences
4   Running workshops, open mic session and love-ins

5   Running a summer school, short course or retreat
6   Running a magazine or Web site
7   Running a listserv
8   Organising a political rally
9   Starting a book club or review-writing club
10 Fixing a prize for an old friend

Okay, maybe not the last item, but working with people to develop something for the broader community repays your effort tenfold. Get working.

17. What to Say to Everyone

As we discussed earlier in the book, maintaining a mailing list is extremely important. You may use it to keep you and your concerns at the centre of people's thoughts. Here are some observations and a word of warning. Some poets maintain personal mailing lists which they use to manage their status within a community of "friends". Email addressed to "Dear Friends" always seeks to establish the writer's attempt to build consensus around his of her vision of how the art should proceed. Even more, some poets may use the consensus of a community to carefully judge their own concerns, adopting them in order to align themselves with a political current.

I've never felt comfortable with consensus building or the gentle warmth of convention. Poetry, like all arts, and politics, can suffer from the newsworthiness of its deliberations and concerns. Chasing some issues can appear not just opportunistic, but profoundly inauthentic. Take care in circulating emails on the latest famine, earthquake or political outrage. Still, one can spot such tendencies and the poet can make as much use of them as she or he can stomach, especially when wishing to court the generally centre-left hegemony of most poetry communities. "Reflecting" in this way, can be a powerful technique, and con men use it to great effect, as do mediums, priests and anyone wishing to control people through their desires and self-images.

18. Working within the Small Press Scene

The small press scene, which I have heard referred to (affectionately) as "small press sludge", can be a fascinating and frustrating world. Insular and amateur, and not necessarily in a negative sense, small presses can become places of devotional activity. They can also be propagandist and progressive, even when such trajectories can look hackneyed and retrograde. They are also ghettoes. Nevertheless, it is an important stepping stone to work with and support the small press scene, to discover allies and practitioners who are trying to sell books and promote the writing they love.

You'll find the haughty, the holy and the wholly ludicrous, but most, if not all, are possessed of the clear desire to find readers and converts for their vision of poetry. Few are interested in money, even less in genuine book sales. Occasionally, someone springs from the scene to become a mainstream player. A lot of small press psychology is built around low-tech solutions and giving access to local talent. Most small press devotees are the engines of a local writers' circle, centred upon a fugitive magazine and often upon an individual. Almost all small press activists support their circle with remarkable zeal but lack, or denounce, the commercial infrastructure to take their writers beyond a small audience of peers and aspirants. For some this is their justification, for others it is a muddle of anti-capitalist sentiment and should be taken, lightly, for what it is.

Nevertheless, most poets build their reputations from the small press world of chapbook publications, leaflets, magazines, postcards and, increasingly, CDs and audio product of all kinds. The sheer size of this world can be daunting, a huge expansive base at the bottom of the pyramid of the poetry economy. Small press publications can also become the evidence of significant poetry movements; the publications surrounding the New York Scene in the 1960s are fascinating, delightful and occasionally compelling products. However, the poetry economy, like the world economy, has moved into new arenas, and it seems increasingly unlikely that small press publications can have the same impact as the underground did at the time of the social revolution of the '60s and '70s.

A good way to begin with the small press scene is to start a magazine. More on that later.

19. Using Bulletin and Message Boards

Bulletin boards are the places the lonely, desperate or egotistical go to avoid too much self reflection or lapses in self esteem. Well, at times it can certainly feel like that, even as one participates in the scraps and exchanges, as well as the wonderful messages of support and sense of community. Bulletin boards are also great places for establishing word of mouth and building a reputation. Join as many as you can, and spend as much time as you can muster, joining in. There are, by and large, two modes of interaction: initiators and reactors. Initiators provide or provoke debate whilst reactors attempt to police or temper the conjecture and hyperbole.

20. Residencies

From football clubs to prisons, café bars to universities, poetry residencies have proliferated since the mid-Nineties. Poets can be expected to write upon the delights of cappuccinos, the merits of mid-fielders, or the ins and outs, though mostly ins, of the penal system. Residencies may be managed by third parties and involve some form of application. Some are advertised. Most involve a modest commitment of time within a fixed period, rarely more than a year. Activities may include workshopping, running a programme of events, working with others on a project and providing some form of written feedback or documentary evidence of the outcomes.

A key feature of all residencies is participation and collaboration, and the degree of each will largely be determined by the writer.

21. Giving Workshops

Running workshops can be a rewarding occupation for poets, ranging from regular monthly events in smoky cellars, abject provincial libraries, dim pubs and damp squats, to lucrative overseas residential stays on the Med with the workshop groupies huddled on mountainsides basking in lyrical wonderment, drinking Soave and lionising the poets.

The range of workshop experiences is wide and varied for both participants and administrators. Some poets run them (sensibly and equitably) for money, trying to eke a life out of the art in whatever way they can, and you'll certainly earn more from running a regular workshop than from book royalties. Financial rewards from such events could be based on a hand-around hat, through to a short-term contract of employment with a workshop institution.

You may see workshops as community-based activity, or you may see and situate such events in the context of privately-funded higher education. Whichever way you frame your stance to workshops, you'll need extremely good interpersonal skills and an ability to focus on the needs and impulses of other people, and their trajectories as writers. Many people desperately want to be poets, rather than write poems, and their sense of self worth and their "personal construct" may be linked to such an identity. These experiences can be challenging and rewarding, or, indeed, filled with potential conflict.

Your role in this is as an expert in managing writing and understanding the processes of composition and revision, focus and flow, compulsion and consideration. No one can write well who doesn't read well, and your advice may steer people into new arenas, new landscapes and territory for their art. Balancing the critical uptake of poems with the permission needed by aspiring writers to extend, ratify and progress is an art; some do this extremely well, others do not. When one looks at the regular faces running workshops, be aware that this is as much a product of teaching success as it is of some ranking in the popularity stakes. Big names do attract customers to commercial implementations of workshops, but good teaching and good teachers are measured by other means.

Try running workshops in your local area and advertise them in your local library or bookstore. It's easy to locate a free venue to hold your meeting, test your skills, and find those techniques which you can hone. Those techniques can also find a home in your own art as you look at what succeeds in the context of readers' experiences. Once you've developed your skills you can extend your services and offer them to others on a contractual basis. All the while, you are building your profile as an expert and, though your primary focus ought to be on the needs of others, this work will repay tenfold with every workshop attendee becoming a potential referee for you and your writing. A good workshop can change the life of a young poet.

22. Giving Lectures

Many universities participate in running lecture series for poets to meet and greet both English students and Creative Writing students. It's still possible to arrange a lecture tour to visit a cluster of universities, hold a reading, run a workshop and give a short lecture on some aspect of poetry and its contemporary practice. This doesn't have to be framed in terms of theory, though your audience may be attending within a certain context, which may be a fresh reading of Derrida Blanchot, Iser or Fish. Find out about the context of the audience; what are they being taught right now? Build a network of friends and contacts within the university system and talk to them on an annual basis about running a simple session dealing with something relevant to their syllabi and students.

If you are going to allow Q&A sessions for the lecture, make sure these are managed with questions fielded by someone and, where possible, delivered in advance of the event for you to consider.

Lectures can be nerve-wracking, so talk about what you know; you'll feel more comfortable when discussing something familiar. Lectures should provide facts, insights and anecdotes to illustrate points. Always use humour, and remember that most audiences want you to succeed in addressing them and will meet you half way when you try to entertain as well as elucidate. Keep lectures centred around no more than three central themes or concerns; few people can take away more than three ideas from a talk. Keep talks short where possible. Allow half an hour for the main points of your argument, and a further twenty minutes for discussion, and ten minutes for wrapping up and soaking up the applause. Wherever possible, spend time after the event with students who may lag behind to meet you face to face.

23. Giving Reviews

A great way to build your reputation as a writer is to review the work of others. Don't just consider works of poetry. Writing on fiction will bring you larger audiences and introduce your name to a wider community, some of whom may well buy your work. As a reviewer, your position is as a writer and critic and the genre you work in is not significant. In fact, it's far more fertile to hear a poet discussing biography, fiction and science writing. The insights and approach can be rewarding for readers.

Write one review every month, selecting the hottest title of the moment, finding what works with the book, and finding the best means possible to relate those successes to the reader. Reviewing well isn't about you showing off what you know and how clever you are (though this will be a side-effect), it's about helping the *reader* to understand what's great about *this* book, and why they should *buy* it.

If you concentrate on why books should be bought, you'll be the firm favourite of poets and publishers. If you concentrate on some abstract consideration of literature or literary theory, you'll bore the pants off most readers. Tone and pitch are imperative. Look across at other genres altogether to see what has happened in, say, music reviewing, sport or automotive reviewing. Most other industries have adopted a style which is informative and fun, focussing on the reader and not on the doctorate. Reviewing is about talking to people, not about educating them.

Consider reviews at two lengths, 300 words and 1,000, and use those constraints to focus your writing, as well as your target market. Short reviews can find a happy home in small journals as well as broadsheets, larger reviews can find a home in Webzines and literary journals. If the review extends beyond a 1,000 words, it's either too long, or it's becoming an article and your approach should change.

24. Interviewing Other Poets

A fantastic way to build relationships with your peers, and especially to develop your skills as a writer, is to conduct interviews with other poets. The scope for publishing interviews has expanded massively, and the Web can provide a wide range of opportunities to publish your interviews; you can even post and host them yourself. Few poets will reject the offer of an interview, even if it doesn't lead anywhere interesting for them. Most interviews are conducted through email, though some are face to face.

Thanks to the internet, it's relatively easy these days to locate poets and to approach them. The interview needs a context and that context must be relevant to the work of the writer, but it could be focussed on ecological themes, translation, performance or new work. Find that angle and explore it with the poet, allow the questions and themes to evolve in a few emails and then write down the three things you'd really like to know about the writer; the three absolutely essential things about why you're fascinated by them. Start there and then extend the questions in relation to the poet's responses. Follow your nose and your notes. Get something of real interest, and remember that people are fascinated by people as much as by product, so don't forget to introduce your interview with a short biographical summary, not a curriculum vitae, but something like, "So, you're living in Kansas now, what's that like for your writing?" Get inside the writer's life.

Interview at least three poets a year, and if you're not hosting the articles yourself, build a reputation with a Webzine to locate and market the work. Circulate information about the interviews widely, get the author to post a note on their Web site and post links on every site you can find which deals with the writer.

25. Writing Articles

Consider writing articles on poetry and poets, as well as related fields like teaching writing, or managing creativity, or using writing within some other application, like therapy, rehabilitation or personal growth. An article should deal with a broader set of issues than a review, but you should still consider it a piece of journalism. In many of these marketing ideas, we're extending your thinking about your professional life beyond being a "poet" to being a "writer", someone who is capable of using words in many ways to address readers on many subjects. Turning your hand to journalism means developing relationships with editors. Remember that all editors need to fill their pages every week, indeed, in many cases, every day with material which will entertain and engage their readers. Readers, as in *circulation*, is the name of the game, and your writing should be topical or offer a fresh perspective on your subject. It may be controversial or polemical, but your writing must never leave the reader cold. We want to be stirred, even if it is through violent disagreement. Talk to literary editors at your regional or national quality newspapers about what you can offer. Send in an example or two, link your writing to their current interests and, most of all, know their work. Read other columnists and test out voices for your writing. Adopt different registers for your own writing and see what happens. Once you have a foot in the door, send in pieces on a regular basis, regularity and timeliness are critical factors. Never let up. Never let down.

26. Running your own Webzine

A great way to establish an international base of contacts is to run your own Webzine— an online magazine of poetry and reviews. Avoid accepting submissions in the early stages, instead contact people whose work you admire and ask for a contribution. Build a profile for the magazine based on the quality of contributions as much as the profile of the contributors. Keep in touch with contributors, try and establish a range of regular features, regular writers and, of course, a regular readership. Writers often have a pecking order for their work:

- quality broadsheets and weekend supplements
- national printed poetry magazines
- regional printed poetry magazines
- major online journals and poetry portals

and then, somewhere at the bottom of the heap:

- Webzines

Unfortunately, Webzines can often help to perpetuate that pecking order, through awful Web sites which may be intended to convey the underground or alternative nature of their endeavours. It's not unusual to see Webzines launched as the vehicles of a small community or clique of writers, some may contain ill-considered selections of friends and colleagues, all wrapped up in a kind of amateur scattiness, self-referential material and in-jokes. Do not fall victim to this kind of approach, and keep the trajectory serious and aspirational. Live up to those aspirations. Put work into context, and select work which sits well and reinforces each writer. However, what's interesting about this pyramid is that it is changing. Writers are beginning to recognise that a decent Web-based publication has a far greater out-reach to new readers than articles in print. Web publication is a form of global syndication and, what's more, it can be easily referenced and linked to as the world of the writer begins to grow with the world of her or his readership.

27. Running your own Blog

This book cannot do justice to sheer explosion of life writing which blogs comprise. From the adoption of digital personae through to a diary of undigested morsels of experience, exchange and personal narrative extension, blogs are quite simply a new phenomenon and still in their infancy.

Blogs can have an explosive effect on the reception of a new title, offering a more powerful way to engage with and stimulate word of mouth than any other medium I know. However, it is exceptionally difficult to disseminate and direct information through blogs. They are, in the best senses, unmanaged, and if there is a genuine uptake of your book, this result can be a wide and fast-paced exchange of news and links. In a matter of days, the viral nature of blogging can take your title around the world and back several times. For example, when an extract from this book was picked up by blogs, visits to the Web site doubled in two days.

Blogs can appear to operate in one direction, but it's not uncommon to see blogs used as a form of exchange and it's this form of syndication which is of most interest to you as a writer.

Starting a blog is free and all it takes is time to produce new material. The reader's experience of a blog is to get a regular feed of new ideas and experiences, all from the horse's mouth. Once you start, you can't afford to let it slip. You have to feed the meter. Your readers may visit while new content is being hosted, but blogs can fade if nothing new is on offer. Keep yours up to date and make sure that you write something at least once a week, and preferably every day.

Some blogs become a phenomenon, for example, Ron Silliman's blog at http://ronsilliman.blogspot.com/ and can achieve quite staggering levels of readership, far broader than some national newspapers. The quality of writing and the range of concerns is critical to stimulating that readership; it is the power of the columnist transposed to new media. Whilst we pause for thought on that, let's not lose site of traditional media.

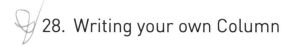

28. Writing your own Column

A traditional newspaper column can be a powerful mechanism for discovering and engaging with a print readership. It's also a great tool for self promotion and provides a captive audience for everything you write elsewhere, including your poetry.

A column might evolve from a weekly investigation into themes and considerations surrounding poetry or literature in general, or it may deal broadly with culture or creativity. If you've built a reputation up as a reviewer and author of feature articles, running a column may be your next stop. However, it needn't be too grand.

Try your hand with your local newspaper and offer to write a column on ideas and imagination, the city's or region's cultural events, or subcultures. What new books have appeared? What do you see emerging within new writing? How does your city feature in terms of national cultural output?

Whatever direction your column might take, it can advertise you and your writing and provide a platform for supporting others and their art, whilst helping to develop new communities of readerships for the writers you admire and would like to see more widely-read.

29. Working with Special Interest Groups

Whether it be an evening with the Friends of Coleridge Society, Help the Aged, or the Kansas Mortician's "Verses of Glory" Collective, you can offer a programme of activities which addresses the needs of the group.

You may approach groups with proposals for discussion and debate, examining the continuing impact of Banjo Paterson, or contemporary readings of Blake in modern London; the possibilities are endless. Constructing a programme of readings and contributors can be a fantastic way of introducing your work and its influences to new communities.

There are thousands of appreciation societies, primarily for dead poets, and there are always local interest groups for local poets, whether these be dedicated to the Romantics in the Lake District of Cumbria, or the Walt Whitman Society of Long Island. Think creatively of readerly and performative interpretations of other poets and write suggesting a programme of events.

30. Working Within the Arts Administration

Lots of poets are inextricably linked to the arts administration, whether this be through trade bodies, government bodies or those administrators linked to endowments and private sector grant-funding bodies. Each of these communities has a highly-developed language and set of behaviours for dispensing patronage. Most writers are interested in the money aspect of this patronage—largely defined by the poor pay, or no pay, poets can expect from publication. This economy is largely determined by such conditions, and its effects can reach beyond the practitioner into the publishing world. Many publishers are funded, too. Even beyond this, distribution may also be financially supported. Even beyond that, a lack of audience may lead to further tiers of administration working on the development of readerships and these too may be funded. The only people who aren't funded are the readers. This has led to a peculiar economy which needs to justify its existence outside of demand, often in terms of "culture"—though it is hard to imagine an authentic culture which has no demand.

It's important to learn how to navigate these communities and reflect the language in order to gain access to the networks of contacts. Money can be important, but focus attention on gaining access to audiences. Success in pleasing audiences can and will lead to greater support within the arts administration. Audience, or readership, is the nirvana of all arts administration. A secondary range of concerns will oscillate around race, gender, sexuality and social inclusion. Be prepared to discuss your work in these terms.

A further tier will form around topical ethical, religious and social concerns: ecology, sustainable communities, religious tolerance, religious oppression, land rights. Such topical concerns can be clearly seen in the relationship of the media to government. Keep a weather eye.

31. Getting an Internship

Which sounds like finding the shortest way into the State Penitentiary and can feel like that for some interns. A great way to build relationships is to gain an internship with part of the poetry community, whether this be within a poetry collective in a city or a magazine, Teachers & Writers or even a publisher. You might find work in helping to run a venue or supporting a Webzine. Whichever direction you move, this is a fantastic step for the novice and the expert to extend their contacts and build friendships, to nurture writing and at the same time develop the relationships to sell your work. Internships are an important, perhaps vital, part of the poetry community. Write to a director offering your services and be prepared to work for nothing for at least a day a week. Activities will nearly always be at the coal face, often the grunt work of sorting things out. Good interpersonal skills are vital, but good research skills can be invaluable, too. Identify every arts organisation linked to poetry and poetry funding in your local community and offer your services. Keep a record of everything you do, and build your CV. Keep a record of everyone you contact in the poetry business. These are your future collaborators. As an intern, you are selling yourself first and foremost. You should be a positive, though not exuberant, problem solver.

32. Making Literary Friends

Though it sounds banal as well as manipulative and false, forging literary friendships is an important activity—not purely for personal gain, but for the timely support it can offer and that welcome ear at moments of sheer desperation. There will be a few of those.

Sharing your work with literary friends can help to weed out trite poems or hone belters.

Some poets, like some hip-hop artists, find pleasure in personal enmities, trashing the opposition at every opportunity—which can seem a natural extension of the passion and integrity of personal practise (well, there may be money laundering and extortion attached, but the poet laureate isn't really a yakuza, as far as I know).

If you are Kool Keith, dissing someone can be real funny, but if you aren't, choose your literary enemies carefully. The world of books and writers is a small one with a long memory. You never know how power will end up being shared out or controlled. You may not care, and this may be your drive towards the delights of the underground. Beware of the underground, it does not offer a superior form of poetic validation; mostly, it offers sewers and soil pipes.

Despite the fun and games of giving someone a ribbing, there is also plenty of solace to be found in virtual communities—it may be hard to distinguish a coterie from a support structure, and there may be little to separate them in terms of their behaviours; some have power, others do not. Don't be distracted by the politics. Friendships may form the basis of a movement, or nest of vipers, but they do count for the developing writer. Still, friendships separate you from people as much as they unite you, so be generous and supportive of your colleagues, as nothing will extend your opportunities more than a helpful hand from an acquaintance at the right moment.

So, should we concentrate on other poets? Well, no. It's good to have literary friends in as a wide range of areas as possible. Booksellers, critics, programme developers, academics, gallery owners, the list can be extensive. A circle of friends can form a positive international community who will be active supporters of you and your writing. In fact, the more you act within this broader community of critics, media moguls and party life, the more you'll gain some unique insights, be appaled, and have some fun.

33. Working with the Community

We've explored ideas of internships and working with local services and local media and we've talked of the poetry community, which is better understood as a plurality, with often widely differing concerns and trajectories. But it's also important to look at the broader community and consider working with schools, hospitals, libraries, and indeed every aspect of local infrastructure.

Think of hosting readings and workshops, festivals, holiday events, talks for children and parents about poetry and being a writer. Look at village halls and parish councils. Take every opportunity to evolve the role of poet as a touchstone of the local community: someone to turn to for advice and information, ideas and access to creativity and freedom. You might run a children's day on "Spells, Incantations and Curses: An Introduction to the Black Art of Poetry."

The thing to remember is that the wider community is where the real poetry readership lives, and coming into contact with them can act as a check and balance from shop talk with one's peers.

34. Maintaining your CV

Just as with your efforts to obtain gainful employment, it is important that you maintain your poetry CV. This isn't a question of inventing successes and skills, in fact most business CVs appear to unravel when confronted by a few questions from a potential employer. Where poetry is concerned, stick to the plain facts.

Your CV will list who you are, where to get hold of you and what you have done in reverse order. Organise the information into sensible sections: Employment, Residencies, Internships. Readings, Festivals, Prizes, Bibliography.

You will use the CV to sell your services to most of the people you come into contact with, for example, when writing to editors or potential collaborators. Keep the CV to two pages and make sure it is succinct. When listing important things like the work you've done in the community, list the two or three key successes of each post as bullet points. These can be discussion points when talking to a panel, feed them the things that you are confident talking about, and which demonstrate the range and depth of your experience. Concentrate on your people skills, your ability to work as a team player and on your performance skills as a poet.

35. Maintaining your own Bibliography

Many poets fail to maintain an accurate and up-to-date bibliography of the books they have published. I find this rather shocking. It's a bit like turning up a Blazin' Bob's Bowling Emporium only to discover you forgot to put the kids in the 4×4, and have left them on the porch at home.

Keep a careful record of every poem and where it has appeared, and a list of every chapbook, volume, anthology and edited work you've written or appeared in. This will rarely extend beyond two sides of paper, but get it right. Bibliographies have some clear rules and *The Chicago Manual of Style* provides detailed guidance on constructing them and reference lists. If you don't have a copy, buy one.

36. Working with Professional Bodies

It does no harm at all to approach professional bodies for support for your book. Most national poetry societies offer news about new publications and some will host launches or run free email alerts. Some organisations will highlight authors with new books, and may ask you to wear a red ribbon at a conference or supply a note for a newsletter. Make use of all offers to promote your book.

Some organisations work harder than others. The best I've come across so far is Poetry Ireland—I've never come across a cultural body that worked harder to launch and support writers. If you want to discover what they do, write and ask to join their mailing list, and check out their Web site at www.poetryireland.ie/

Contact all trade bodies and ask for help and advice, you'll get it in bucket loads and every bit will be valuable. Stay in touch with people and, where possible, attend events and get to know folk. Find out who manages events, who organises newsletters and mail shots. Who is the regional advisor in your area? How often do they meet? What local events are there? Professional bodies are there to support their members, so don't forget to join. Active members are much more fun to work with than passive ones, so once in, play a role. Ask what you can do to help in your area.

37. Using your Local Library

Local libraries are fantastic places to promote poetry—high art or low, a library can be a fun place to gather people and poetry together and can form a natural extension of a community of readers and writers. Libraries are there to serve us and support us, so talk to your librarian about organising reading events, running a reading group, holding a poetry workshop, or for example, running a high school programme like "Libertines, Terrorists and Vagrants: Poets in the Twenty-first Century". Find new ways to draw people into the art; operate on a wide range of levels. Run a parent and children's day, introducing poetry to the young "If Bunny's Bounce, Do Frogs Flounce?", or something cheeky like "Limericks and Lingerie: An Afternoon of Poems":

> I once had a bra from Havana
> whose cups were made out of *tobacca,*
> suffice it to say
> that I smoked it each day
> sipping rum with St. Benedict's vicar.

Okay, not my best, but you can do better. Hold a local poetry competition in the library. Hold annual events in the library. Talk to your librarian about a programme and talk to the local community about potential events. Invite poets from out of town, have an afternoon of songs and ballads, or a focus session on indigenous writing, or use the resources of the library by having a research programme on poetry and anthropology. Have all cultures at all times produced poetry?

38. Using National Libraries and Archives

The United Kingdom maintains a national deposit. Make sure you book ends up in the copyright libraries. Many national libraries have a special collection of contemporary poetry. Check them out and ensure your book is in the collection as researchers and anthologists often make use of archives and it's important to have your work included.

Many national archives are moving online and extending their collections to digital and audio product, offering a wide range of products and services for free. Check out such collections and write to offer your book and recordings. Get involved with the head librarian or chief archivist and find out everything you can about the collections. Some libraries run extensive mailing lists offering news and updates on acquisitions and events.

Many national libraries are actively involved in canon-building, finding ways of clearly and exhaustively representing the cultural outputs of the nation. The Poetry Library in London also maintains an expanding online, searchable collection of poetry magazines; a truly fantastic resource for poets and readers to discover what is happening in the world of poetry. Have your name included in every archive you can.

39. Getting into Directories

With the ceaseless expansion of the internet, reference sites are almost boundless. Many have almost completely replaced print directories, so write to every directory you come across which lists poets and their work and ask to be included. Be shockingly promiscuous in taking your name to every site possible. Don't be worried or upset about being rejected. Don't be too pushy and strike a balanced and friendly note. You're simply asking the directory manager to give you some help in listing you. It's difficult to reject a request for help.

40. Don't Ignore the Young

If you ignore the young, your readership will die in your own lifetime. If you aren't prepared to talk to the young about your work, changing tone and register as appropriate, then you can't expect to develop your audience. Most poetry is sold to women who are currently over fifty years of age. That's a diminishing market and there's no evidence that succeeding generations are joining this age group with a new interest in poetry. If you want readers, start with the younger generations. They're your pension plan.

41. Handling the Fans

Wear body armour and carry some baby wipes. Actually, fans are fantastic, and make the whole enterprise worthwhile. Enjoy your fans and, if you can, offer a chat room to meet them on your Web site. Always give fans your time and follow up on leads and conversations. If someone gives you their address, write to them. Nothing sells books better than a fan base, so take time to give your readers everything they need to get in touch, stay in touch and discover what you have in the pipeline. If you like this book, let me know. If you have some other ideas you think work well, tell me about them. I'm keen to learn— we're all in the same boat, finding readers and selling books. You can reach me at chris@saltpublishing.com.

3

Sorting your Book

Y ou've been busy building your profile, preparing the way for all your books. The process of building profile never really stops. Here now is a short chapter on some aspects of sorting out the product, so that it's right for the market.

This is firmly your publisher's territory, and they will be working with the trade to get everything right. If you like to interfere, to maintain control, to have the final artistic say on font, paper, printing, cover design and the weight of cover board, then publish the book yourself, you don't need the experts. You'll only have an unhappy time letting the publisher, sales team, wholesalers, head office buyers and shops develop things to make your book a success. Best to avoid all that, if you know what it should look like.

If, on the other hand, you want to participate and support the experts, then learn to use the expertise of others and allow them to transform your book from a wonderful manuscript to a wonderful product. The team will need your help, so support them, but don't demand control over things. Be prepared to accept the fact that *your* book is now *their* book, that's the deal, and their part of the contract is to convert your product and *you* into saleable goods.

 42. Your Book Cover

Nothing is more important in achieving sales success than the cover of your book. Contrary to popular opinion, you *can* judge a book by its cover: if the publisher, author and increasingly, bookseller, have failed to develop a successful cover (one that makes you pick up and buy the book) you can safely assume that no one thinks the book is worth bothering with.

Like any author, you will have ideas about what the cover should look like, you may want to supply an image, you may love cerise, or taupe. You may enjoy looking at pictures of zygotes, race horses or kittens. However, developing a cover doesn't have much to do with your preferences. If they happen to coincide with what the market expects, that's great. If not, you need to abandon your dreams of the cerise kitten and spend time looking hard at what sells in your local bookstore. Be prepared to have a say, but not to direct the outcome of the cover design. Be prepared to hate the cover, but also to understand that it fits the market.

The best place to start with judging covers is to look at the competition. Your cover is *not* working in a vacuum. Wander in to your local bookstore and look at every cover on display in the trade fiction and literature section of the building. What's on offer? How do the books look? You're bound to see some trends in cover design. Like any area of fashion, cover design is driven by emulation and consolidation, as well as by differentiation, and, above all, fashion.

Some books demand certain covers. Poetry is certainly more flexible than IT manuals and cookery books, but poetry is often linked to the appearance of trade fiction. Every Western publishing nation has raised the stakes and invested more and more time testing cover designs with focus groups and a wide range of corporate staff, as well as central book buyers within bookstore chains. Indeed, for many trade titles, it's not unusual for the bookseller of a major chain to have the final say on a cover, or to demand it be redesigned. No one has a better understanding of what draws someone's attention and gets them to lift your book from among the hundreds on offer in shelves, spinners and shop windows. If in doubt, test your cover with a few booksellers.

Book buying decisions are made in around 10 seconds. Think how much information you can take in in 10 seconds. The important factor is the *emotional* impact of the cover—the "sell" is a *visual* sell. Any cover text merely reinforces or supports that visual trigger—confirming the subliminal decision of the buyer. It's the cover design which establishes the *desire* to purchase.

It's worth spending time looking at the big publishing houses to see what they're doing. Go online and visit the web site of Bloomsbury, Faber, Norton and Random House. Spend as much time on the cover as necessary to get it right. Live with a cover for two days before committing to it. Ensure that the right people have made the decision, or have approved of it. You can kill a good book with a bad cover. No book will recover from a bad cover, unless you redesign it and reissue the book.

43. Your Photograph

The second most important thing about your cover is your photograph on it, or on the Web site to accompany the book. Very few poets enjoy the fact that people buy authors and not books. However, the two most important factors in any publishers editorial strategy are author base and subject specialisation. For the poetry publisher, the most important thrust in marketing is to develop the writer's persona and sell that to the public. Fame counts. Most of this book will deal with pushing *you* front of house.

In a culture obsessed increasingly with celebrity, Goffman's work *The Presentation of Self in Everday Life* can certainly be a touchstone for how poets must assume personae, or have them foisted upon them, for the purposes of literary consumption. Read that book and consider how your behaviour will work within the world of poetry.

Back to the snaps, ensure you have the best possible photographs taken. Build up a store of photographs and locate these on a Web site for easy access by publishers and the media. Your photographs will tell stories and it's important to take time to develop a range of narratives within the images—a visual writer's biography. You won't be fully in control of these narratives, but understanding how they work is key to managing your presentation to the reading public.

(Upon seeing any images, customers will begin to narrate their sense of who you are and what you stand for.)Beware of avoiding the use of self-imagery as an absence of photographs can build distrust between writer and reader and you may be seen as untrustworthy, secretive and aloof. Here are some tips on making images work:

1   Think of photographs which *authentically* convey your writing life and its "drama".
2   Make sure that the photos are large, sharp, have good contrast and are high resolution (if using a digital camera, ensure photos are saved as 300 dpi JPEGs).
3   Choose a strategy in taking a set of publicity shots, treating them as a project. Will you be building narratives about you, your current work and its location(s), or will you be using studio shots focussed on your appearance?
4   Think of using interesting angles, locations, close-ups, activities, humour and surprise. Play around with images.
5   Pull together sets of photographs and categorise them.
6   Don't use holiday snaps or family photos.
7   Don't use camera phones.
8   Avoid shots with too many people.
9   Take time to crop a photo. A good crop can make an image.
10   Treat your representation as creatively as your poetry.

44. Getting the Right Title

I've published some books with titles I'd rather have dropped. We all do this. Writers can feel such a degree of ownership over titles, images and layouts that one wonders why they aren't self-publishing the work. It's important to trust the market where titles are concerned. There's no hard and fast rule, but memorable titles often tend to be short and pithy. Long titles, unless they are surreally compelling, tend to be instantly forgettable.

If you want a good test, think of the bookseller trying to remember and order a title for stock. The number of times I've heard people say, "it's the book with dreaming something in the title" has left me in no doubt as to the merits of brevity.

I've watched customers in stores give up in desperation with trying to remember complex titles. Keep it simple. Take time to get the right title. Let the title address the book and avoid things which have no relationship to the work. Don't be too clever. Test titles out on people. Discuss it with your publisher. If they don't have a view, there's something wrong.

45. Each Book Sells Every Book

Never forget to use each book you're publishing to sell previous volumes. Consider a page "Also By" facing the title page, listing all your work. Remember, in any publicity, to call back to previous work:

"Grace Benson is author of the Oklahoma Book Awards' shortlisted poetry title 'Perfect Level of Risk', and of the bestselling memoir 'Saving Grace'."

Use your books to sell everything you have written, as long as you stand by those works. Even if you move stable, your publisher will be happy to support you publicising all your titles. The collective pressure of a body of work is an important marketing tool. Use it.

Nevertheless, be careful of using statements which overstate, inflate or simply cause incredulity:

"Colin Teams is fifteen years old and is author of forty-two books of poetry and over one hundred chapbooks. His poems have appeared in thousands of journals from *Axle Bum* to *Noxious Winkle*."

46. Finding Endorsements

Endorsements are the responses of the great and the good to you and your work as it is developing, and especially to your latest production. They are distinct from descriptions for your book and from review quotes, but may appear alongside these on your book's cover.

Do endorsements work? Yes, if you trust and know the endorser, so choose who endorses your work carefully. Endorsements from within a coterie will only support the coterie. Endorsements from wildly inappropriate sources will undermine your product:

> "Kimble's poetry is on target and on message. It hits you like a bullet, and the lines hook you and draw you in"
> —*Fishing and Hunting News*

It's not an uncommon mistake to think of getting endorsements from unusual folk to address new markets, but I'd be extremely careful about this. If your local restaurant was offering endorsements from iron foundries and rubber stores, you'd hardly be persuaded of their Bouillabaisse.

Your publisher can help you find endorsers and can approach them too on your behalf, if you'd prefer that. However, don't just say to your editor, "I'd like my endorsers to be Seamus Heaney, John Ashbery and Les Murray—thanks." You should do some leg work and find people who (a) have an affinity with your work, and (b) would have the time to support you.

Many people refuse to endorse books for reasons of time, accusations of nepotism, or the thrall of indebtedness. As you build a reputation you'll experience the same pressures, with everyone under the sun asking for a few words for their cover. How you manage that is your business, but helping to sell someone's work you admire is never a mistake.

Get the length of endorsements right: less than seventy words, preferably less than twenty and, in some cases, no more than a phrase from the right place. Brief the endorser. Look at how the system works for fiction and trade paperbacks:

"Unmissable!" —*The Times*

"Burning excitement!" —*The Independent*

Such endorsements can seem commonplace on books splashed with "THE NEW NUMBER ONE BESTSELLER". However, these devices do work to place a book in context and actually talk to the market in a highly-informed way—the language of endorsements is precisely that. There are things to be learned from such techniques and a well-placed, memorable endorsement can help people to make the all-important decision to actually look at your work, rather than race past to the next book which does shout about its virtues. This might seem hard-headed, but the general public actually do read book covers and use the information to make an informed purchase.

Above all, avoid turgid or gestural endorsements which mean nothing and say nothing:

> Eliciting fabro-technile dependencies and Saussurean phantasms, Roche's liminal banquet is more behest than promise. Experience the fictive tics and languishments. Flesh is cursive dependency. Art is savage oil. It is yours now. Endeavour to divide amongst the vestiges. *Remplissage!*

It's not uncommon to read stuff like this on covers, especially of avant-garde works, however here it is the poetry that is intended to be pushing the art into new terrain, not the blurbs. No one can be convinced of this form of vouchsafing. Who is being addressed by such an approach? In many cases the endorser is writing for their own readership, writing into and out of their milieu. Don't let such concerns distract you from seeking clarity from your endorsers.

Remember that although the scope and trajectory of a work may have its friends and accomplices, the readership should, indeed ought, to extend beyond the confines of such communities and be addressed in a language they can understand and in terms which grant them access to the work. In other words, an endorsement should never be a barrier.

47. Pacing Yourself

As a general rule of thumb, you should avoid producing more than one volume of poetry every six months. Don't laugh, it's not unknown for me to have published a book by an author only to discover another is on its way elsewhere inside three months. Over-publishing kills good books. It simply drowns them. Consider pacing your career in three-year intervals. This allows books room to breath and gives publishers at least thirty-six months to actively market and sell a new work.

If you are producing work on a faster scale than this, it ought to raise the question of quality for you. It certainly raises a question of logistics: don't expect your publisher to be issuing books with less than three-year gaps. Importantly, select your work on that basis, letting the best work to rise to the surface, and allowing ideas and compulsions to take shape, gestate and find successful realisation. You're not pacing your writing, which can be as fevered as you want it to be. You are pacing the likely engagement of your readership. Don't exhaust them.

48. Writing Descriptions of your Book

All books have to be described to readers. (As we have discussed, this is different from endorsements and review quotes, which offer a reader's take on the text.) A book has to be described to say clearly what it's about, what it deals with, what it consists of.

Some people find this process rather onerous. As professional writers I cannot see why the task should be too tricky. All you need to focus on is the simple question, "What's it all about?"

Write two descriptions in the third person:

1 250 words in length, where you can explore themes and concerns, the shape of the book, and address readers with genuine subject interest in you and your writing.
2 A shorter version of around 50 words, aimed at the novice, the bookseller and the busy buyer.

Your publisher should make use of these descriptions in all publicity. They may alter it.

49. Understanding your Publisher's Distribution

A great deal of confusion can centre around how distribution works. Ordering and shipping books can take time and effort. Announcing to your publisher that you have a reading tomorrow night in Wisconsin is not especially helpful. Talk to your publisher about turnaround times.

Another common issue around distribution is payment terms, and account status. No publisher likes supplying books which are never returned nor paid for. Most book distributors will require that customers open an account. They may seek a credit reference, they may demand payment up-front from people who do not wish to become regular customers. They may only supply on minimum order values, minimum quantities, or seek a firm sale (not allowing returns to be made).

Some non-traditional venues can be inexperienced in placing orders; I've seen reading venues wanting to sell books ask for a hundred copies, mainly to please and impress the poet, but only manage to sell one copy. Recognise that publishers and their distributors are businesses that need to protect themselves against bad debts, amateurs and enthusiasts.

If you are doing readings and performances in non-traditional venues, the publisher's distributors may not be able to supply. In these cases, you may want to let the publisher deal with the venue direct, if they have time and can make that work. Alternatively, you could take books yourself, which always ensures delivery and puts money in your pocket.

If you're planning a tour and want books, plan their despatch with your publishers well in advance. No one wants to be paying courier bills for books to arrive late.

50. Rewriting

It's a good idea to have finalised your text *before* you submit it to your publisher. Nothing is more frustrating than wasting time rewriting an entire book once it is in production, causing delays and confusion. Editing and minor textual changes are inevitable, but don't embark on a complete rewrite of the text, or submit a host of replacement files for every other poem. Get it right first time. Spell check everything you write, and *read it*. Better still, get someone else to read it and give you feedback on the text. There's no such thing as a perfect book, but poetry publishing isn't a form of continuous publication. Once you've handed over the manuscript, the process of writing has ended, the process of editing and marketing has begun.

51. Seasonality in the Market

Most US publishers work off seasonal lists, Spring and Fall. If your book is a gift book or anthology, the main Christmas selling season will be important. Are you writing love poems? Then St. Valentine's day is a perfect time for seasonal promotion. Adoption cycles for courses can lead to sales in May and September. Don't push a title between semesters unless you aren't selling to students or academics. Think of seasonal events which can best support marketing pushes. Make offers when the market is stagnant, but don't make offers when the market is buoyant.

52. How to Kill a Good Book

The worst sins are over-publishing and disappearing acts and for those two things you should go straight to the ninth circle of Dante's *Inferno*. There's nothing better than publishing two other titles in the same year to ruin both. Disappearing is great, too. Especially when publishers have planned and allocated resources for two years, lined up reviews and interviews and you've fallen off the radar.

The next two sins are refusing to perform the poems and refusing to help sell the book, that gets you into the fourth circle. Always ensure you are available for interview, for journalists, producers and reviewers. Be willing to run with the publicity, *always* follow up on leads, and be on time for every performance.

53. Understanding the Process of Publishing

It pays to understand as much about publishing as possible. About the functions within a publisher, from editorial, marketing, sales, production and design, warehousing and distribution, rights, finance and, of course, publicity. It pays to understanding the processes that a text goes through, from review and contracting, proofreading, editing, endorsing, typesetting and design, correcting, the development of electronic product, physical printing and binding, shipping, storing and distributing. Oh, and handling returns. It helps to understand the efforts of everyone involved in the publisher and the book trade to getting your book out there and making it sell. Briefing the sales reps, convincing the retail buyers, convincing the wholesalers, designing the best cover with your trade partners, finding the right price, and discount, the right balance of resources. Learning about publishing can be a lifelong journey conducted in a dramatically changing landscape, sometimes a landscape in turmoil. Don't be ignorant of the context of your writing, and especially of the real size of the market.

54. Timing: When to Publish

Some markets are highly seasonal, so be prepared to choose the best time for the book. That might not be your preferred time, but it will be the best date for the highest sales. Publishing at the end of December is too late for Christmas sales, too late for folks to have much disposable income, and will potentially kill the book. Publishing your book when Seamus Heaney is launching his will not offer you much chance of space in the poetry columns. Don't launch in August, as everyone is away on holiday. Spring can be good, as people feel they can shake-off winter and are ready for all things new, and the Fall can be good as long as it's early enough for lecturers to mention the work on their reading lists and for hard-pressed students to choose literature over beer and their debt repayments. Each country has some seasonality, so work with your publishers to time things right. No point publishing if you're going to be out of town and out of touch for a month. No point clashing with another major literary event. Check out everything when planning the date and your marketing plans.

55. More on Author Photos

Visit the Web site of your favourite band and check out their publicity shots. Look at the locations, the drama, the quirkiness, the irony, the use of shadow, angle, colour, the narrative splendour of celebrity, creativity and cool. Now reassess your plate photos and see if they measure up. Do you look like a potato? Do you look like the school dinner lady or the maintenance guy over in 13B? Take some care in appearing to be what your readers desire.

4

Selling your Book

et's get down to business. You've prepared the way,
you've worked with the publishing team to get the product right for its market, now it's time to start selling. In
this chapter we'll look at a range of tools and techniques to sell
the book; some are grand ideas and some are really small. Our
job is to begin investigating all the processes we can use to
stimulate interest, find readers and sell them the book.
Marketing and sales are a matter of lifelong learning. Don't
stop with this book, read as many books as you can on marketing and selling, but stick with those that are plain, direct and
focussed on "doing" skills. Avoid too much theory. The best way
to gain access to the theory is to see what works for you and
examine the successful processes to see what led to the
winning formula. Pick and choose what works for you. Some
things may seem trivial or trite, but give everything a go, and
see what fits for you and your personality. The most important
tool is belief in the product; from this all sales will flow.

56. Writing your Press Release(s)

The press release is an important tool in promoting your book. However, don't think that there should only be one. Keep them coming.

A press release isn't a list of facts, nor is it a list of endorsements, descriptions or selling points. Don't let your publisher issue an advance information (AI) sheet as a press release. A press release is a *story*. It must have impetus, it must be newsworthy and it must grab your attention in the first line. Above all, it should be *interesting*, a simple and crucial word.

The story must have an angle and this is what you should spend time on when working on the text. Some press releases wholly arise from the angle—fitting the story to the event. Some press releases need to find an angle to bring them to life. Be sharply aware of the opportunities to write a press release, actively seek them out, and write them throughout the "life" of your book. You can never under-publicise your work.

Whatever you undertake, work closely with your publisher to produce this—not because you'll co-write it, but because you'll want to know how to jointly handle the responses. Of course, some publishers have the benefit of a publicity team working full-time on their lists, but not all poetry publishers enjoy such resources, so chipping in will help. Never surprise your publisher.

A great many press releases end up being used to fill column inches. In a media hungry world, content is king and a press release can provide useful copy for a pressured team of journalists. It's not unusual to see a press release used verbatim. The better you are at writing copy, the more likely your piece will be used. Don't forget the story.

Remember that the press release will have an audience beyond newspapers and news services. Sure, you can use a press release to announce a book, or relaunch it on the back of a feature but you can also use it to approach special interest groups. A press release can significantly extend a marketing campaign—everyone loves a story. You can deal with negative issues as well as positive ones in the story, but don't use the item for a hard sell, just tackle the issues. The sales will come from the growth in interest. Don't forget the story.

Consider the audience for the press release, and tailor it. For example, your local newspaper will probably want to focus on the human interest angle of a story, and your copy should aim at highlighting your life and the events surrounding your publication. Put as much effort into writing the story as you would a poem. Don't forget the story.

At the end of writing your press release, check the spelling. Check the thrust of the piece; each paragraph has to count. Add notes for the editor on whom to contact for more information and don't forget to include the ISBN, price, extent, format and publisher for the book. Oh, and one last time: don't forget the story.

57. Twelve Simple Steps to a Decent Press Release

The following notes summarise how to draft a press release, especially one suited to Salt Publishing. A thoughtful, dynamic, well-crafted press release which follows these guidelines will gain the attention of journalists and is perfect for distribution through any publisher's press office.

1   *As we've said, the story is everything.* If there's no story, there's no news. A press release is not an advert. Sexual misconduct, prize management, controversy and madness all sell literature, though I don't advocate the pursuit of such things.

2   *Answer the reader's basic questions.* A successful story answers all of the "W" questions (who, what, where, when and why) and one "H" question (how).

3   *Smash and grab.* Your headline and lead paragraph should summarise the story and completely grab the attention of the reader.

4   *Write for the reader.* Many media outlets, especially online media, will print a press release with little or no modification. Write the story exactly as you would like it to appear in print.

5   *Paint the picture.* Use real life examples to explain what has happened. Contextualise and show proof of any outcome. Give examples of how the story fulfils a reader's needs or satisfies their desires.

6 *Stick to the facts*. Tell the truth, avoid hyperbole. Never try to flannel the journalist or reader. An exclamation point is proof of incompetence. Keep the tone neutral, incisive and strong.

7 *Get the right angle at the right time*. Timing is everything in finding an story. Constantly look for current news items, social or political issues which could drive a press release. Ensure your story has a "hook". Old news is no news.

8 *Use an active voice*. Use an active voice and verbs to enliven the press release. Use strong verbs to convey emotion.

9 *Brevity serves clarity*. Use just enough words to tell your story. Avoid unnecessary adjectives, heightened language and redundant expressions. Reduce the story to the bare essentials without losing any interest.

10 *No buzz words*. Never use literary jargon, dialectical thinking or business speak in a news story, unless you are debunking them.

11 *Get permission for all quotes used*. Or spend your life in disputes, or court.

12 *Check your spelling, punctuation and grammar*. Unless you wish to advocate illiteracy.

58. Getting Broadsheet Reviews

Most poets will devote a lot of time to considering reviews. Most poets want the validation a review can give. Most poets love a good review, and will sustain a personal vendetta against someone who pans them. A great deal of attention is paid to how many reviews one receives, their depth, support, intellectual engagement and general rapport. Is it all worth it? No, not really.

It's not really helpful to provide your publisher with a list of sixty broadsheets and journals where you want review copies to be sent. For most poetry titles, the cost of sixty review copies and their postage will wipe out the profit, so it's imperative to be selective. One can send notice of the availability of review copies, but carefully target people and places who may be supportive of the writing and its trajectory. Literary editors have fierce loyalties and fierce enmities. They are at the centre of a political machinery, trying to navigate through power bases and the sources of advertising revenue, as well as trying to find the truly interesting, truly engaging book. Literary editors will follow trends, so it's not unusual to see the same book reviewed in a wide range of broadsheets. Is this because there is general agreement upon books to be reviewed? Or the power of the publicist in the matrix of relationships within the trade? Literary editors have thousands upon thousands of books to wade through every month. How will yours stand out?

It's important to note here that, contrary to popular opinion, reviews don't sell books—they build profile. Most poets will focus their attention on the validation and credibility they can enjoy from a solid review. However, most publishers will want to focus on sales. The two don't always match, and the cost of reviews is borne by the publisher. A terrifically small amount of reviews can wipe out the profits of an entire book, so be judicious. More than that, be clever.

Sending out blind review copies is rarely a successful policy. The trick is to forge a relationship with a literary editor and with a host of reviewers. This may sound like a fix, but it isn't. It's not uncommon for a regular reviewer to approach the literary editor with the idea for a piece. Some reviewers have particular cache with a literary editor and may make regular contributions to a broadsheet. Building a support structure, as in most walks of life, is a matter of patronage and *Realpolitik*.

Find people who will support your work and who might be encouraged to review it. Work with and through people rather than across or against them. You may find this system uncomfortable, but recognise it and use it for what it is.

59. Giving Away Free Copies

The gift culture permeates the poetry world. In the main this is because few poets earn a living from the sales of their work and few publishers focus on sales as their primary income. So much of the world of poetry is built upon "funny money", patronage and the intensely well-meant funding of foundations and public bodies.

However, poets may earn their work from being a "writer", and a free gift can be a nice way to open doors and introduce yourself. For some poets, this sense of sharing and building networks is a key part of their sense of vocation, participation and collaboration. However, it comes at a price.

The easiest way to give dispense with your profits (and those of your publisher) is to be excessively generous with free copies. Where poetry is concerned, books aren't cheap and postage certainly isn't. Plan carefully who should receive frees and know why they should receive them. If the reason seems lame, send them a postcard instead. People prize what they pay for, and if you can convert acquaintances into customers, everyone benefits; books are valued, your publisher receives income to run their business with and publish more poetry, and the writer receives more royalties.

Nevertheless, using free copies is a good way to raise interest and spread the word. *Always* follow up your gift with an enquiry as to how the book was received. Wait two months and send a note. Did they enjoy the work? Was it challenging or rewarding? Giving a book as a gift is your expression of interest in the views and taste of the recipient, so make sure you canvas their response. Most importantly, make sure you ask everyone you send a copy to if they know of anyone else who might be interested in your work. Never be afraid to ask for help in finding new customers. As long as you are sensible about the funding/cost of free copies, you can help to create word of mouth and some new sales.

60. Poetry Competitions

To my knowledge, Walt Whitman, Adam Lindsay Gordon and Christina Rosetti didn't win any poetry competitions. Don't mope about if you don't. You shouldn't expect to be treated fairly, or expect that prizes will lead to unending celebration of you and your work. There are more than a thousand poetry competitions in the English-speaking world, ranging from the best poem on the theme of liver, to the best haiku on the topic of pet insurance. Their cash value, prestige, notoriety and sheer range of celebration are dazzling and absurd.

The culture of competitions can be perverse, occasionally spilling over into fist fights in the broadsheets and with Web sites dedicated to the uncovering of prize-fixing and nepotism. Much of this stems from the naïvete surrounding how the poetry world works. It all makes for great copy and poetry never gets so much attention as when there are accusations flying around about the uncovering of a new Star Chamber, guilty of ensuring that most of the latest shortlist took a dive in the third round.

Last minute changes to the rules, changes to the judges, resignations, retribution, friends awarding friends the same prizes year in and year out—it can be super fun to watch. Is everyone laughing all the way to the bank? No.

You'd think poetry was awash in high-value prizes, cash spilling over the trestle tables of the judges as they smoke cigars and knock back the bourbon, laughing at the country cousins who have paid good money to take part in the imagined "meritocracy". Well, fun though these images are, poetry is *not* a meritocracy, though no one is getting seriously rich. The money really isn't the issue, but the validation and the valorising are. You will need to negotiate this. It's best to be realistic; whistle-blowing tactics certainly won't cause a clean-up of the acts—well, not in the long term.

Poetry is a small world tending towards insularity and some-times bitter fragmentation. It's not difficult for anyone to be compromised. It's not difficult for anyone to be corrupted, you included. It won't be long before you know many of the players, and they will know you. This doesn't excuse the imbalances and injustices about competitions, but we ought to see them in their context. Most competitions are used to fund poetry busi-nesses, for better or for worse.

Prize-winning poems are often heavily derivative and strike all the right notes for the judges. I don't know of a single instance where a success here also constituted a major work of art. So let's not confuse the two. A prize-winning poem will contain all the right references, be fashionable, use the permit-ted diction and prosody of the time, and contain few surprises or disruptions for its middlebrow market. It will be worthy, perhaps even earnest. It will fit the bill.

Take time to consider the judges and their predilections. Search out previous winners and runners-up and check out for patterns. Take note of the relationships between previous judges and the winners; research their writing, research who they are endorsing. Most of all, work out the template for success. Make a list of the competitions you want to target and prepare poems for submission. Successes can be used to promote your last book and prepare the way for the next. Make sure that your biography incorporates the successes, too. We'll deal with this elsewhere in the book.

61. Mailing Out Postcards

Postcards can be produced extremely cheaply, everyone loves receiving them and you don't need to open the envelope to get the message. They're perfect vehicles for spreading the word and reinforcing your publicity and are a powerful and cost-effective means for generating sales. Send out at least a hundred. Handwrite every one, *personalise the note*, and watch the responses come in.

The postcard should be of your cover and it must include details of your ISBN, the title of the work, your name and the price. It might also include the number of pages and the trim size of the book. It ought to identify your publisher. It should be full colour. Most importantly, it must provide a Web address for people to go and buy it.

62. Placing Adverts

Does advertising work for poetry? Not in the way you might imagine. Splurging your hard-earned wonga on a single ad in a decent broadsheet or journal will have little or no impact on sales—the key lies in repetition. In fact, it's hard to relate the impact of advertising on sales of products at any level, or for any corporation. Having said this, it's true to say that advertising is absolutely vital for preparing the space for sales to be made. Avoid advertising at your peril.

If publishers are footing the bill, few authors would show disdain for a well-placed ad on their behalf. However, if you want to consider placing your own advert it's important to understand how things work. Advertising creates a cultural space of *potential* of new (life) choices— it ploughs the field for the seeds to be sown.

Remember that the point is not the product, but what the product symbolises in terms of personal status and sense of self-determination and self-ownership. As we conduct our lives in a huge sea of choices, choices about how our lives will gain meaning through *acquisition*, poetry has to compete within the same cultural theatre. This isn't to abandon your anti-capitalist credentials, if you have them, but it is a recognition that in order to offer your message to potential readers, you have to operate within the visual syntax of the day.

People are very sophisticated in dealing with visual messages and few are ever convinced by advertising to buy against their interests. But few will buy at all if you cannot compete with the stylistic range and complexity of other products or lifestyle choices—both in terms of adding value and being representative of, or reflecting, the sophistication of the purchaser. Betraying the brand betrays all those who have consumed it. Poetry advertising must compete, evolve and become more radical in its approach to the spectacle of contemporary life. If it is to subvert, enlighten, provide solace, rapture or transcendence, it cannot succeed if it lacks sophistication, credibility and emotional power and engagement. Products, like ideas, have to be presented before they can be grasped.

On average, you need to repeat things nine times before getting any form of response. On this basis, advertising can look expensive. Checking out rate cards may provide you with a bank-breaking, debt-ridden future. If you want to go for it, here are some pointers:

1 Consider ad sharing and ad exchanges, especially if you run your own journal.
2 Start negotiations at 70% off the rate card price.
3 Look at bulk discounts over six to twelve months (your campaign will change shape after one year).
4 Plan your campaign out month-by-month to maximise the impact and integration with readings, events and reviews—timing is as important as repetition.
5 Unless you are a trained designer, don't produce the ads yourself.
6 Don't focus on the cover or endorsements, focus on the visual and emotional aspirations of the reader.
7 Fun is a very important sales tool. Truth and earnestness are dull friends in the shop.
8 Less is more. As a poet, your tendency may be to let the language do the work. Resist this, let the image do the work—imagery has longer shelf life in the emotional memory of shopping.
9 Avoid what is customary, conventional or plain cheesy.
10 Tiny ads tell consumers that you are either poor, cheap or half-hearted about what you are trying to sell them. Remember, customers buy through association.

63. Working with your Local Bookstore

Your local bookstore can be a huge ally in helping to "break" your book. Booksellers are always on the look out for something that their customers will want. There are no boundaries to stretch here. If you want to help sell your book, you should check out your local bookstore and find out about book launches and poetry events. At the same time, get a feel for what the manager thinks of poetry in general. Okay, that will take three seconds, and once you've recovered from the laughter or the blank expression, you can find out why poetry doesn't sell and talk to her or him about what can be done.

Listening to your bookseller can be a wonderful and painful experience. You don't need to apply the advice to your creative life, but it can be sobering to hear about what people want, and the bookseller knows from personal and financial experience what sells and what doesn't.

Many chains now run "open mic" sessions for local poets and support local publishing activity. Over the past few years, bookstores have opened coffee shops, supported later opening hours, offered a wide range of events, book signings and sales offers—are all part of the bookseller's portfolio of sales weapons. Getting people involved in the store is the principal way to combat online sales and their impact on market share.

You can help the bookseller draw in a new audience by offering to run events or supporting those that are in hand. Many bookstores also support literary festivals, helping to run events during the year and manage the festival book sales. Explore these ideas and build a relationship with the store manager and the poetry buyer. The time will come when your title will be drawing the crowds.

64. Marketing at Book Fairs

Book Fairs are terrific places to market books. To get the best out of them, prepare your days well in advance. Stalls are static and reactive, so use them carefully, if at all. If you can, find someone to take messages at your stall. If you are sharing a stall, rotate your cover.

At least two months before the fair, identify exhibitors, potential collaborators or customers and contact them to arrange a meeting. Allow 45 minutes for each session and 15 minutes to get to the next. Fill your days, allow no space. You can always squeeze someone in if they turn up unannounced and strike you as a sales prospect.

If you do have a stall, make sure that no one is trapped at it all day (nothing is more boring or disheartening). The key to a successful book fair is mobility and meetings. Drink lots of water, avoid alcohol and too much coffee. Eat light. Get fresh air outside three or four times during the course of the day.

If the book fair is an annual event, build contacts and plan meetings a year in advance. Touch base with as many of last year's contacts as possible. If some people have proved important in the past year, arrange to have lunch.

All the deals will be firmed up after the book fair, so don't worry about pressuring for a sale on the day. Use the book fair to make and manage your contacts and above all to *listen*. Take business cards and catalogues and exchange these at every meeting. Place your appointment's business card in front of you—it will keep her or his name in front of you, and later, will remind you of who you have met.

If you get caught in an unproductive meeting, let your diary set you free. Full days of meetings provide plenty of opportunities to excuse yourself. Dress smartly, not too loud, not too casual. Look attentive and give all your attention to your appointments. Smile, no one buys off a misery. Avoid making any financial commitment on the day, but list potential orders where you can. Set yourself a target to develop ten new leads and ten new sales. Keep notes and write up each day's events in the evening in the form of a list of actions to be taken. It's easy to forget opportunities at a book fair, and the list you compile will provide you with a plan for the next month, and perhaps the next book fair.

65. Selling at Unusual Venues

Which sounds like pushing poetry at what the British call a "car boot sale", but is actually about recognising that poetry and its audience are unpredictable and to be found in unusual locations. Don't expect that all poetry sales can or will be made to the cognoscente at readings and festivals. Music venues, art galleries, independent cinemas, libraries, comedy stores, theatres, museums, clubs and bars all provide alternative spaces to find book sales. Each venue brings with it a slightly different audience, but one who may share an appreciation of cultural artefact; this should be exploited. The audience for poetry needs to be recreated, and the natural constituency for poetry is a liberal arts crowd. Some venues may provide a shop —galleries often do—and others may have room for a stall or display. Producing flyers, leaflets, leaving catalogues or post-cards can all help lead to a sale. Beware leaving any books on unmanaged displays, as for some, the temptation may prove too much and books may wander. Finding alternative venues for poetry sales is an important part of redeveloping audiences.

66. Selling at your Launch

Many poetry publishers are ceasing to hold launches for books. This is partly because the task of arranging a launch is time consuming (and therefore expensive in staff time) and partly because it is increasingly difficult to recoup the costs of food, drink and a booked venue from the poetry sales on the night (or even beyond). If you want to hold a launch, work closely with your publisher in making arrangements. Here are some tips for helping to ensure the event pays for itself.

Avoid Monday, Friday and the weekend. Ensure that the event starts early evening after working hours to avoid a double commute or dead time between finishing in the office and getting to the venue. Make sure that invitations are clear that the event is to sell books and celebrate your new work. Consider charging for tickets to the launch, the cost can be offset against the cover price of the book. Alternatively, consider stating that each invitation gives you a discount on a signed book at the event—this may encourage sales.

Readings should last no longer than twenty minutes at a launch, with anecdotes. Introductions at a launch should be light in touch, merely welcome the guests, mention where the toilets are, where the food and drink are, the poet, the title and where everyone can buy the book. Provide a stall and display which people can clearly see. Allow time for book signing. Allow time to meet with guests, chat and pick up any leads on where and when the book might be further promoted. Ask people for their thoughts on where else to market and sell the book (get them involved).

Above all, have fun and enjoy the event. Plan where the launch party can move to, line up a local pub or restaurant for people to retire to after the event. Move people on after two hours, if not before.

67. Soliciting Reviewers

As we have said, the best way for publishers to flush their profits down the drain is to send out too many unsolicited review copies to the benighted leagues of literary editors. Think of all the junk mail you have ever received and how delighted you were in opening it all up and reading it. Yes, I'm sure that the tens of thousands of books sent out are all carefully considered and not for a moment lined up on the floor in scores to cast an eye over the sea of mediocrity and finally settle on the covers which don't look like a dog's dinner or the author's attempt at a memorable image.

If you want good reviews, it pays to seek them out. This doesn't cut across the work of the literary editor and their independence, rather it supports them in helping sort those books which are actively supported from those which ought to have remained unpublished. Gaining the support of a decent reviewer can help vouchsafe a book through the frighteningly competitive world of reviews. Remember that obtaining one good review is better than sending out one hundred copies to achieve none. Scale is not important, quality is. In terms of sales, remember that a broadsheet review is no guarantee of that stock-clearing order. Web reviews are even less successful in terms of sales.

The tone of a review is vitally important. It's debatable whether the style and slant of some reviews actually assists the reader in being drawn to a work, rather than be made to feel inadequate before the intellectual onslaught. The music industry has, it could be argued, travelled through such excesses, and is confidently readable and supportive of fans and customers. You would do well to seek reviews which test out a variety of registers, and help readers to find and buy your work. It may be heresy to say so, but the purpose of the review ought to be sales driven, and should centre on the "sussed" reader.

68. Working with Festivals

There are hundreds of literary festivals, some dedicated to poetry, most to the serious money associated with trade publishing. Some may support fringe activities, some are entirely comprised of fringe activities. Festivals can help to break a talent, in both senses of the word, but the fact that you have or have not been invited to participate should not lead you to the absinthe.

Some poets are festival groupies and may excel at the crowd-pulling, crowd-pleasing systematic pleasure of the professional reading—this is neither a commendation or condemnation of such skills; it pays to be able to perform. If you're crap at it, get better. If you hate performance and have night sweats at the thought of speaking to the milkman on Friday morning, you might be in the wrong line of work. Performance is now an unavoidable aspect of "being a poet". Practice it. A lot.

Some poets are festival administrators, helping make arrangements and planning the gigs and booking venues, managing the accommodation, the drunks, the hot-tempered, the disappointed, the vacant, and the dissident—that's just the poets. Festival directors, like many others in the literary world, are affected by fashion and funding, so breaking new talent or new poetry is bound to be risky and testing. You'd do well to recognise that festival directors are clever and serve a base of customers who may not share your personal vision of art.

Money chases conformity, just as hastily as it does success. Breaking new ground means you are leaving your compatriots behind, so don't expect to find an audience, you will bring one with you, and it is this readership which will interest the festival director, as well as the money which may follow. A festival is judged on ticket sales. Most directors are willing to take small risks. Share your work with festival directors, get involved in your local festival and, above all, attend festivals to see the audience as much as the performances.

Some festivals are inadvertently hilarious; I've seen performances which drifted, bizarrely, into mock Scots accents. I've seen performers fall from the stage, not drunk, but terrified at the prospect of an audience. I've seen a glass of wine swiped by an unfortunate gesture of welcome into the front row. Once you're on stage you're there to entertain folk, so do your best to achieve that; don't overstay your welcome. (And everyone corpses once in a while.)

Select the festivals you think look the most promising for your work, categorise them A and B and send your book and a CV listing your performance history. As festivals are interested in ticket sales, your marketing should focus on how those are to be achieved.

69. Using your Family, Friends and Colleagues

What else are friends and family for but to exploit for the achievement of higher book sales? Now, this may be the motto of the cynic and the rake, or even your agent, but selling your granny to boost sales can be fun.

The truth is, friends and family can be of tremendous use in spreading the word and finding new leads to chase up as potential sales avenues. Don't count family sales as real, they're not part of your move towards world domination of the poetry scene. Keeping in touch with family, with old teachers, professors and lecturers, with pals from gigs, pals from short courses and poetry love-ins can be useful. You'd be surprised just how many ideas can spring from asking the question, "Any ideas how I can sell more of my book?" So don't forget to ask that of those closest to you. Keep a list of those ideas for the next book.

70. Book Signings

A kind of valediction. Book signings are about saying goodbye to members of your audience. Think carefully about what you want to leave people with. Final impressions, like first ones, can linger in the memory for a long time. Treat everyone uniquely, ask them about their take on the book, ask them if they enjoyed your reading. When preparing to sign, ask the person's name and write in carefully on a separate sheet of paper to check the spelling. Then write the name in the book. Many copies have been spoiled by a misheard name or an error in the spelling of "Jayne", "Stephen" or "Toni".

71. Using Internet Bookstores

As we've seen throughout this book, the internet and the World Wide Web are now central to the writer's participation with their audience. This revolution has changed bookselling, too. It's not possible for bricks and mortar independent book-stores to have infinite range and depth of stock and they are facing increasing competition from supermarkets, chains, and online bookstores. We'll deal with this later, but for now, inter-net bookstores are only going to increase in number and in the range of services they offer. For convenience, it's hard to beat online book buying. Online reviews are extremely powerful ways of signalling public interest and the polling most stores offer can be an important indicator to book buyers of the real value of a work. For example, we distrust politicians, but trust the letters pages of our local paper. The wily activist can use this to create a more "real" uptake of political ideas and pres-ent them in a way which are readily consumed as "fact". This is also true of online reviews; we're more likely to read and accept book reviews by real people than a *TLS* or *Boston Review* treatise on meaning and value in contemporary society. The rise of the amateur review is a powerful incentive to sales. Check out how independent music finds its audience.

Pull together a pool of readers to review titles online, includ-ing yours, and build the impression for other customers of hot titles which have real merit. Avoid taking the cultural high ground in such reviews, or attempting to reveal how clever you are in your late-capitalist, post-structuralist reading of the text. Your aim is to create a sale. Reviews work best when they simply say how a book changed you, surprised you or delighted you, how the book represents a development for the writer (thus pointing to other books and creating a second wave of sales), or how the book succeeds as a work of art.

72. Small Press Book Fairs

If you want to see the face of the small press scene, at least once, then book fairs can provide a close-up glimpse; so close you can smell its armpits and count the nose hairs.

Finding the right quality of material can be tough going at times, but you can also be surprised by beautifully-crafted product, some of which surpass their content. Many miss their markets because of the crafted nature of such endeavours, but there are genuine sales and real customers to be had at small press books fairs. Small press consumers are also big press consumers. The differences are primarily economic expectation and publishing experience. Many make the common mistake of thinking that publishing is primarily production, where for most large publishers, production is merely a means to an end; the end being profitable sales.

Look out for ideas and contacts, make friends and talk to everyone. Beware of hulking individuals who stand for too long at the corner of the trestle table, especially those with pockets full of poems, along with bus tickets and alarmingly large handkerchiefs.

73. Preparing an Online Questionnaire

Prepare sixteen questions which a lay reading group can use to to discuss your book to stimulate conversation over the hors d'oeuvres and Chianti. Sixteen questions which don't require a masters in cultural theory or in depth knowledge of prosody.

Most major trade publishers are providing online resources for reading groups. Prepare yours and offer it to your publisher, as well as posting it on your own Web site.

Take time to consider which questions which would provoke discussion of your latest work, its themes, concerns and trajectory. What should people expect of you and your work? What will people gain from the book? How does the book hang together? You may be exceptionally skilled in considering these questions and capable of framing them in the context of literary, political or social theory, however, avoid that kind of discourse and focus on your personal motivations in writing pieces and the needs of others. Who you are, why and how you write this, are the three most fascinating initial questions for the general reader. Think of questions which will provoke discussion; what readers want is to be led into a debate where they can express *their* ownership and judgement of *your* work. That is the source of their power and entertainment.

74. Using Word of Mouth

Quite the most powerful tool at your disposal, word of mouth is the largest driver of poetry sales. More persuasive than a £1,000 advertisement, more successful that a £40,000 branded promotion of panel-selected new talent, more effective than a dozen reviews in the best broadsheets—word of mouth is the nirvana of publishing success. Tap it and you'll sell more books than by any traditional marketing means. It is self-generating and self-perpetuating.

Word of mouth is simply the product of human exchange. It is non-professional, non-corporate and tends to be unmanaged. Many publishers however will exert considerable pressure to convince potential readers to spread the word. They'll seek out where there are access points to word of mouth: writers' circles, readers' groups, literary blogs, bulletin boards, customer reviews at Amazon.com and of course, through public libraries via literature and reader development programmes. Publishers will coax and support such activities, offering readers' resources and guides. No one who is serious about publishing can seriously avoid dealing with word of mouth.

The World Wide Web has unleashed entirely new ways for people to discover and trust the experience of others. This includes the power of blogs or bulletin boards to circulate news on hot new titles, the online questionnaires and author portals, and the sixteen questions comprising the free readers' guide available as an online resource. The Web has extended the ability to reach and resource new audiences, faster, cheaper and more productively than ever before.

So powerful is word of mouth that many publishers are switching away from traditional marketing to further embrace a direct relationship with customers, developing programmes, performances and activities which deal directly with readers rather than with the trade and the more traditional arena for publishing reception: the literary and cultural broadsheets and their professional critics.

This phenomenon has had some unusual side-effects. The role of critic has perhaps been diminished in recent years and the role of unprofessional reviewer has grown enormously. It's interesting to consider the future role of literary journalism in light of these profound changes, but one thing for certain, the canny author can draw upon resources to bolster their impact by word of mouth. The poetry scene is a vast network of relationships, and by using those relationships to pass on information about your work, you can compete more aggressively than many publishers. They just simply haven't time to devote to building momentum. What they can do is provide resources. Web links to questionnaires, blogs and online reviews are all important. Providing readers' guides and author information is vital. Just as the world of film is occasionally rocked by a strong word of mouth based internet campaign, so too have other industries, the music business, and trade publishing.

Here are some things you can do to help spread word of mouth:

1   When contacted by a supportive reader, ask them to review the book on Amazon or on their blog.
2   When giving workshops and readings, ask people to spread the word for you; tell their friends and colleagues.
3   At events and performances, ask people to contact you for more information on the book. Take time to reply to those that do.
4   Offer to discuss the book with local readers' groups.
5   Contact your local library to offer to come to talk to people about your work.

6 Discover the location of all local readers' and writers' groups and offer to come to talk to them for free about your book and being a writer.

7 Contact your local university and offer to come and talk to students about your writing life and their aspirations for the future.

75. Getting Hold of Good Publicity Shots

Look at the publicity shots surrounding cinema, the popular music industry, sportswear, television, classical music, fiction writing, theatre, corporate promotion—everywhere you look, the pressure on quality publicity shots has raised our expectations of how we expect people and products to be shown to us. Is it cool and creative to have no publicity shots? Is the absence of good visual imagery a useful form of resistance to the relentless commodification of experience and selection, choice and consumption? Even the revolution needs good publicity shots, and poetry as a genre can look extremely poor in relation to the visual breadth of our modern cultural experience.

Spend time pulling together the best shots you can of you and your work. Photographs of you in performance, on the street, in your study—close-ups, action shots, in deep shadow, in broad sunshine—build a whole collection of imagery about yourself, create an entire narrative about you and your writing. These photographs will be invaluable in helping to publicise you. Host the files online in a virtual "press pack", combining information about you and your work, tour dates and contact information. Add a short note about what your work is about, something which a busy subeditor can crib when announcing news about your shortlisting for the Griffin Prize.

76. Getting Information to your Publisher

Most poets, upon publication, forget to tell their publisher of all the work they're doing to support the new book. They forget to mention the new reading series they're taking part in, or that tour the Calouste Gulbenkian Foundation has arranged for them. They forget about the letter of interest from the festival director or the email from the journalist at *The Sunday Times*.

Remember that your publisher is your partner in the promotion of the book and has at their disposal other additional means to support what you're working on. This might include opportunities to add review quotes to their Web site, or host free downloads of MP3s, or simply include links to your new Web site, or that interview you've been asked to give.

Keep your publisher up to speed with all your work. It can help to promote your book and it can cement the relationship when considering your next manuscript. Publishers love poets who can self-publicise, however they're uncomfortable with self-aggrandisement. Avoid asking for resources your publisher can't offer: backing the next tour, personally hand selling your book at the AWP conference. But do keep your publishers up to date with the facts surrounding the promotion of your title.

In addition, when you change your mobile, or phone, or relocate to another state or county, remember to let your publisher know. It's extremely frustrating when one has a lead to chase, like the chance of a radio slot, only to discover on ringing the poet that the line has gone dead.

77. Getting Covers into Online Stores

We discussed just how important covers are earlier in this book. Once you've got the best possible cover, make sure that it appears on every online store. No one likes buying things they can't see, and the online store is one of your most powerful allies in finding international sales.

The book trade has adopted a single standard format for transmitting cover images, a 648 pixel high (or wide, whichever is the greater) JPEGs, saved as RGB and at 100 dpi. Some vendors require a 72 dpi version. Support both flavours.

If your publisher hasn't managed to get your cover onto every store, then they're signalling that they don't understand how the book trade is beginning to work. Sales (especially of poetry) are moving exponentially and irrevocably from high street bookstores to online stores. This trend is unstoppable. There's nothing simpler than generating a digital file for a cover. Make sure it happens.

Initial covers should appear at least five months in advance of publication so that buyers can appraise the title for their stores. Where possible, review quotes from uncorrected bound proofs or late endorsements should be added before going to press. Covers are circulated worldwide through bibliographic agencies and wholesalers, like Nielsen BookData, Bowker,

Baker & Taylor, Ingram and many others. Talk to your publisher about how they handle this, and make sure that your personal schedule allows for the cover to be prepared as early as possible after contracting to allow for pre-publication sales promotion.

78. Going On Tour

Pack light and move fast. That way the missiles will hit air, and you'll be screaming up the asphalt before the exits have been blocked.

Well, okay, going on tour as a poet isn't quite the camper van, Jack Daniels and groupies experience many aspiring artistes might fancy having a go at, it's more a case of damp evenings in some Burnley social club, drinking mild and hoping at least one other person will turn up to make it a threesome. Poetry readings can be a little lean when it comes to audience, as you'll no doubt discover.

However, planning a tour and organising the logistics of making a visit, having dinner, dragging some books to a venue and raising your spirits long enough to knock the audience dead, *can* be great fun. Not all tours match the British experience of immersion tanks and sensory deprivation. Some venues have a real audience and you may be surprised to find scores of young and old eagerly waiting for you to blast them away with some high-octane material. In general, turnout within a university-based reading event can be higher than those gigs based around writers' circles. The first rule of engagement is to recognise that the venue is all important, both in terms of its track record for live literature and for turn out. The second rule is timing. Friday night at the local poetry reading doesn't really compete with a night out on the dance floor or knocking back pints of VB in your favourite Melbourne watering hole. Wherever you are planning your events, in the western world, Friday night is binge night. Avoid Mondays, as everyone will be grizzly from weekend hangovers and the first day back in the office. Tuesdays and Thursdays seem to work best. The next rule is to work with your organiser.

The emergence of performance poetry has done a great deal to develop new audiences for work which delivers digestible and accessible work centred on shared experience, wit and occasionally minority experience, whether that be religious, sexual or racial experience. The emphasis is on entertainment, telling rhyme and rampaging delivery. The model isn't dissimilar from the Eighties comedy stores; crowd-pleasing tactics have to be felt through a shared ethos and shared ethics. These can be challenged. The conventional (and inaccurate) take on performance poetries as being weak on the page has given way as performance has become a genuine issue for all poets.

No one can afford to deliver their work badly now. For each tour, develop a single programme and stick with it, refining the content of performances in line with audience feedback. Modify and develop your routine rather than replace it with different material. Be a crowd-pleaser.

79. Establishing your Thirty-Second Sell

Anyone involved in sales for more than a day learns that people have very low attention spans and, where consumption is concerned, great filters for working out what does gain their interest and, eventually, their money and time.

Where bookselling is concerned most, if not all, buying decisions are made very fast indeed. A book may get around thirty seconds. If you can't say what's needed to sell your book in thirty seconds then you'll miss out on sales. Practise it—it's about ninety words. Work out what people will want to hear to gain their interest and lead to a sale. If you can perfect that, you can deliver it anywhere, anytime. On the commute to work, at the bar, on the bus, in the toilets. Anywhere.

Here's mine for this book:

101 Ways to Make Poems Sell is an insider's guide to the poetry business. It focuses on the issues that matter to writers: building profile, finding readers, and selling books. It offers a frank, funny and insightful tour of the world of poetry publishing. Every step of the way you're offered gems of advice, along with tips and tools you can put into practice straightaway, many of them for free, and all of them geared to getting your books in to the hands of the people that truly matter, your readers.

80. Getting on to National Radio Shows

Radio is poetry's best friend. An intimate medium which enters the mind-space straight through your lug holes. Most radio shows are now streamed over the internet, and national shows have become global. Every country has a national show which deals with poetry. Discover yours. When the time is right, send your book and a story about it to the presenter, and their researchers or producers. You can ring the station to find out who these people are. Always listen to the show and find out about how things are pitched. Like all mass media, radio survives and thrives purely on audience, so your pitch will almost certainly be something that will attract an audience or stimulate the audience to respond. Think of pulling together something that the producers and presenter can buy into, for example, a three-way discussion of a topical poetry issue—war poetry, globalisation and poetry, eco-poetry and climate change, poetry and science, poetry and mathematics. Find angles and curiosities. Send a demo disk in. Most of all, make friends with poetry presenters, as they do a fantastic job of supporting the art and taking it to people who may never have had permission to open a book and discover the art.

81. Getting People to Order from their Local Bookstore

Bookstores have it tough, especially independents. Yep, it's a tough life being squeezed on three sides, pressure on bestsellers from supermarkets, deep discounting on key titles at the major chains, and vast range and availability from the online bookstores. How can independents stay in business?

Well, diversity front of store from the large chains, in depth product knowledge and expertise, and knowing what's hot, can all help. Independents can offer intimacy and elicit high levels of trust from their customers. They can also innovate, offering themed evenings or events and, of course, can specialise in ways that can transform a local store and turn it into a regional or national place to order a given subject.

If you have a local bookstore, support it. When notifying people about the book, tell them that it's available from the store. Send information about your book to the store manager, visit her or him and talk about the book. Organise your launch there and, in any local press release, direct people to the store to buy the book. In the local free notices—in newspaper and notice boards—point people to the store to get your book:

> "Local author Simon Couplet's magical new book, 'Learning to Crawl,' explores our neighbourhood with an eye for everyday occurrence and the forces which act upon us. Change your outlook and buy it now from Sam's Books 1215 E. Bulbeck St."

82. Leafleting

Leafleting is a fantastic way to stimulate sales and it works. There are some tricks to remember. Your leaflet is intended to sell, so include an order form and details of where to buy. Your leaflet will only work if it's better than all the mail you throw out in the garbage, so if your design is cheesy, alternative and low budget, you know where it will end up. Your leaflet has to address people and not hector or admonish them. Above all, your leaflet has to have an offer. People want to know what's in it for them. Are you giving them a discount, a signed copy, a special price, a limited edition or something for free? Whatever you come up with, test it out and pitch it right. Spend more time working out what offer works than spelling out your interest in Stanley Fish, or immanence and the sublime. Your message must be clear, unambiguous and monosyllabic. It will work best if it's also fun.

Leaflets can be inserted in local poetry magazines, left in poetry cafés and libraries, bookstores and reading venues, cinemas, art galleries and theatres. Leaflets can be sent to your friends, associates and collaborators, and can be in shared mailings with other poets. Leaflets can be included in every letter you send out.

Every offer has an end. The end date stimulates the response. You have three weeks to respond. Call me now. Be first in the queue and get this fantastic deal. If possible, use colour printing and use as little text as possible. Make use of a striking image or memorable typographic layout. If mailing, make sure the envelope extends the offer by printing information on it. "Open me now!"

83. Journalism and Human Interest Stories

Marketing is as much about opportunity and timing as anything else. Keep you eyes open and your ears free of wax. Everyday something can present itself which can be tailored to a story in support of your activities as a poet, writer and activist, as well as your actual books. Think about your work and experiences in relation to potential news items.

Almost any event you host can be turned into a story for the local media. Look for human interest angles which feature success over adversity, reinvigorate communities, support the underprivileged, the downcast and downtrodden, or supports worthy causes or social inclusion. Do not be ashamed to find stories which touch the heart strings. Don't centre stories on yourself, but on the activities and participants, the causes and conjectures of the events. Let a few well-chosen quotations ignite the issues and keep the readers interested. Gossip is good.

Surf the local news each day to see what's happening and to see if a story can be written in response to some feature.

84. Building your own Action Plan

Just in case you hadn't quite grasped the shape of this book, don't think anyone other than you is responsible for your life and your work. Your publisher will actively support you, but all books have their moment in the sun and publishers have busy lives discovering new moments to find some income. With absolutely no fault on the publisher's side, resources at some point will be aligned elsewhere, until your next title is ready. To keep up momentum, have your own action plan, split into twenty-four or thirty-six months, dedicated to keeping your thoughts on managing your book's life.

You should aim to give your book three years to do its work and find its readers, at least its first wave of readers. Then turn your attention to the next work and its place in the overall plans for your writing life. Don't have any plans? Well, you'd better start thinking about them as each book should demonstrate a growth of, and new direction for, your art. The better you can plan and envisage that growth and development, the more attractive you'll be to your publisher. The plan is about keeping your writing life productive and focussed. This ensures your marketing and performances have context and meaning.

85. Email Signatures and Domain Names

Email is ubiquitous and most, if not all, of your correspondence will make use of it. You ought to consider buying your own domain: paul@paulrosenberg.com and always make use of your signature to sell your latest offering:

From: "Paul Rosenberg" <paul@paulrosenberg.com>
To: "Dennis Salmon" <ds@knowledgemonkeymag.org>

Hi Dennis,

That's great, let's go with those poems and I'll send you some new material for the next issue.

Very best for now,
Paul

3 Benins Drive, Boulder CO 80302 USA
Tel: 303-498-4991
http://www.paulrosenberg.com

Out now! Paul Rosenberg "The Iron Factory" 0-342-75467-X
Paperback 64 pp $14.95 Available from Amazon.com
More information:
http://www.wolftonguebooks.com/books/rosenberg/

86. One Thing Per Day, Every Day

Not much different from Mao's dictum: "The journey of a thousand miles begins with the first step." Big things are achieved with the drip, drip, drip effect of keeping on writing and working. You don't have to kill yourself to market your book, all you need to do is maintain stamina and be persistent.

87. Setting your own Sales Targets

Never be afraid of setting sales targets for your own books, but only set them if you are prepared to personally achieve them.

You cannot manage what you cannot measure, so if you want readers, set yourself a goal. Do you want twenty new readers before the Fall? Write it down and go and get them. Do you want to sell 1,500 copies of your book over the next year? Write it down and work out how that can be achieved. How many readings can you set up? How many people can you get to those readings? Can you charge and have ticket money deducted from the price of the book?

Setting personal sales targets will focus your mind and your plans on achieving your targets. Be realistic, just as you would with a personal budget. Work with your publisher to plan for sales. Some publishers are only interested in their funding as a means of income, and sales aren't a primary concern. But for you, after writing, sales are everything. Unless you hate being read, or think that the audience for poetry is a matter for posterity. In which case, you're in the wrong job.

88. Using Institutional Newsletters

No university or company I know can escape from newsletters. At times they can look like job creation schemes for listless middle management. Communications Directors may drool over them and the latest demonstration of successful policy roll-out. Human Resources may smile over the latest celebration of the new "Cycling to Work Scheme". However, newsletters can and do reach people within and beyond organisations, and address many thousands of staff, clients and partners.

Use such newsletters to talk about your life as a writer and your new book. Write a little piece and test it out on the editors.

89. Keeping in Touch with your Publisher

Some writers disappear. In my experience, those who do are not interested in selling books or having readers. Some writers believe that the relationship stops once the book is produced. In fact, as this book amply shows, the relationship is just beginning. Contact your publisher at least once a quarter to pass on news of your activities and events. If the book is doing well, a brief monthly phone call on progress will be welcome. Don't overdo it, especially calling every day to ask how sales are going:

> "Yes, Bob, just the one sale. Uhuh. Just the one so far this year. Yep, same as last year, Bob. Okay, yeah. Thanks. Sure, talk next week . . ."

Stay in touch, though, and it's fine to ask how sales are going, but maybe once a quarter. Don't forget to check that your plans match and support the publisher's, too. Make sure that your publisher knows your change of address, knows about that festival you're attending, that prize you've been shortlisted for and the interest from the MFA course administrator over in Oxford, Ohio.

90. Acting as your own Publicist

You can hire a book publicist to work on your title, but if you're like most poets, flat broke, you'll have to find some time to do this for yourself, or watch other books steal the limelight.

Publicity isn't about spending vast sums of money, or expecting others to, it's about finding ways and means of getting you and your work discussed. That process is a daily routine, but formalising how you make approaches and run your programme needs a lot of administration.

In the first six months of publication, put aside a day a week to sit down and work at publicity, using all the ideas presented here in this book, and any you can find in other books dedicated to publicity and book marketing. Simply change hats and assume the role. The more you practice publicity, the better you'll become in doing the job.

Spending money on other trade titles about author publicity and marketing will be money well spent. The more you know, the better. Half the problem is understanding how to behave, the other half is actually doing the behaving.

91. Placing Poems Post-Publication

Start placing new work with magazines and journals immediately following acceptance of your contract. A publishing history is attractive to magazine editors as it shows a commitment to writing, and magazines can provide useful additional support in reinforcing your readership as the latest book hits the shelves.

Where possible, tie in new work with a potential review of the latest book; many editors would see a logical connection in doing that. Offer the book for review if the editor takes some poems. Be careful not to offer poems from the current volume as some editors frown upon taking poems which have appeared in a new publication.

Above all, make sure that your contributor's note includes a reference to your latest work, the title and ISBN.

92. Working with Trade Bodies

The Association of Writers and Writing Programs, the Society of Authors, the Royal Society of Literature, the Poetry Society and many trade and professional bodies around the world, can provide guidance and advice, resources and expertise for poets new and old. Many provide ready networks of practitioners and a wealth of opportunities to forge friendships, share knowledge and experience and collaborate. Working with such bodies can extend your role as a writer into new territories. Join what you can and get involved as soon as possible.

93. Personal Demeanour: Diva, Dunce or Doyen

The biggest hindrance to success with poetry sales is the demeanour of the poet. If you enjoy fist fights and controversy, that's fine. However, the reading public rarely favour drunks, dullards and drop-outs. Your interpersonal skills, looks and appearance are all part of the package. I've attended a reading where we had to bring in security to handle some poets. There are some great stories of punch-ups and drunks falling from the stage. I've seen some poets get plastered as quickly as possible before punishing the audience with a drawling interminable reading filled with self pity and self disgust. They make for good anecdotes. They don't sell books.

If you want people to buy you, they have, in fact, to like you. It's not much different with publishers. It's really very difficult to work with people who are bad at being human, who lack empathy, insight and a bit of levity. If you enjoy making life difficult for others, don't expect queues around the corner of Borders the night of your book signing. In fact, don't expect the book signing. In fact, don't expect the book.

94. Making Bookmarks

Everyone loves bookmarks. Produced digitally, you can find an inexpensive way to give people highly-designed and memorable gifts which remind them of you and your work for months. I have a simple paper bookmark from Waterstone's which dates back decades. The phone numbers and post codes have changed, the company logo has altered — the Chief Executive must have changed twenty times, but that bookmark still gets inserted in most new books and reminds me each time of the shop where I got it and how much I love bookstores.

People have emotional attachments to bookmarks. Produce a few and give them to those by whom you want to be remembered. Put one in review copies or free copies of your book that you hand out.

95. Making Video Clips

There's a new trend to use video online to help sell books. There has been some struggle on format with QuickTime from Apple, MPEGs, RealPlayer and other video formats all competing. FlashVideo has emerged as a new entrant. Consider producing small video samples for your own Web site and the publisher's.

Your video should be short, succinct and highly focussed. Your thirty-second sell will work well here. Check the script, find a quiet location and make the film, just a head or head and shoulders shot delivering the three key messages people can, and hopefully will, remember. Get that clip in place with the book on the Web in advance of publication, or as soon as possible after it. Comb your hair, pluck your nose, shave your ears. Memorise your script and deliver it with conviction in the most natural way possible. Be honest. Honesty shows on camera. Which is why we all trust politicians.

96. Podcasts and Free Content

Where possible, record MP3 files of you reading your work. Have one file for each poem, introduce the poem with an anecdote about its origins or meaning for you. Perform the work, don't read it like the shopping list. Let your voice carry some emotion. Give this content away from free on your Web site, or your publisher's. Offer the material to others who might enjoy and use it, for example, new contacts at magazines and broadsheets, festival managers, venue managers and academics. Offer as much free product as possible. All freebies draw people to your work and the new book. Check out this Web site to see how it works:

http://www.poetryarchive.org/poetryarchive/home.do

97. Supporting Debutantes

A great way to keep in touch with new writing, to refresh your own, and to stay in the public space of poetry, is to work with debutantes. Supporting new poets is rewarding. You can help them by passing on your expertise and experience, you can help your publisher to spot new talent and you can maintain your own position as expert. There are thousands of young people who would like to be poets. Most are interested in some abstract lifestyle choice, a bit like saying you'd like to be an astronaut or lion tamer. But some go a step further and actually strive to write. Working with these people on their developing manuscripts can be exciting. You can hone your own skills as a teacher and mentor, and you can, selflessly, take pleasure in seeing others develop as writers. A by-product will be your continuing connection with poetry and the thrill of seeing where the art is moving, decade by decade. It also helps to stave off the slow death of Old-fart-dom.

98. Google AdWords

The information titan is increasingly offering software tools and services which complement its offer of the world's best search engine. One service Google offers is AdWords, a fantastic way to reach people who are interested in you and your work.

Through keyword-based adverts, you can have your title as a sponsored link. You pay for each click on your ad, and depending on your keywords, you may generate hundreds of thousands of page impressions—the outreach is better than any print media, and everyone who clicks is directly interested in you and your work.

Setting up an AdWords account is easy, and you can decide how much or little you are prepared to pay to have customers go to your Web site or to a place they can purchase your book. Go to https://adwords.google.com to find out more.

99. The One Sentence Hard Sell

This is the only book available which specifically helps poets and poetry publishers to develop sales around the world. Now write yours.

100. Free Supplementary Material

Offer as much free material as possible: posters, CDs, bookmarks, podcasts, interviews, questionnaires about you, new poems, tour dates, blogs, photos of you in performance, links to Web sites which feature you.

Have a place on your Web site where visitors can obtain all this material; make it overwhelming, expansive and fun. Offer it to your publisher, too. However, *don't* give away your books. The tactical use of free material can draw people to you and your writing. It can help teachers and lecturers to plan lessons, as well as help reading groups and writers' circles talk about you. It will delight the fans.

101. Can you Sell Books without Doing any of this Stuff?

Sure, there's a stall on the sidewalk in most major cities. However, if you want your book to succeed in reaching a wide general readership, there's really no escape. Start promoting your work *right now*. Good luck, happy marketing and, above all, *enjoy yourself!*

Index

CPSIA information can be obtained at www.ICGtesting.com
Printed in the USA
LVOW12s1947300315

432577LV00006B/981/P